:RING VINTAGE New York

A Guide to the City's Timeless Shops, Bars, Delis & More

First Edition

MITCH BRODER

Guilford, Connecticut

D1040890

All the information in this guidebook is subject to change. We recommend
that you call ahead to obtain current information before traveling.

Editor: Kevin Sirois
Project Editor: Meredith Dias
Layout: Casey Shain
Text Design: Sheryl P. Kober

Library of Congress Cataloging-in-Publication Data

Broder, Mitch.
  Discovering vintage New York : a guide to the city's timeless shops,
bars, delis & more / Mitch Broder.—First edition.
      pages cm
  Includes index.
  ISBN 978-0-7627-8454-7
1. New York (N.Y.)—Guidebooks. 2. Historic sites—New York
(State)—New York—Guidebooks. 3. New York (N.Y.)—Social life and
customs—Guidebooks. I. Title.
  F128.18.B755 2013
  917.4702—dc23
                                        2013010056

Printed in the United States of America
10 9 8 7 6 5 4 3 2

Contents

For Patty
For King and Mindie

About the Author

Mitch Broder covered New York City as a feature writer and columnist for Gannett Newspapers, the country's largest newspaper chain. He has also written about the city for papers including the *New York Times,* the *Daily News,* and the *Washington Post.* He has won some of the top prizes in New York City journalism, including the Mike Berger Award of Columbia University. Read his blog at mbvintage newyork.blogspot.com.

Acknowledgments

The people who most directly made this book possible are the ones who own, manage, and otherwise tend to the places featured in it. Thanks to everyone who invited me in, showed me around, told me stories, and kept the places going long enough for me to show up.

The person who most literally made this book possible is Kevin Sirois, my editor at the Globe Pequot Press. He liked my idea immediately, guided the project skillfully, and fielded my questions respectfully. For an editor, that's the Triple Crown.

The person who made Kevin possible is my agent, Anne Marie O'Farrell of the Marcil-O'Farrell literary agency. She found the right publisher quickly and has stayed at my side ever since. She is the one who actually got me to write.

Thanks to the authors who offered advice, to the bloggers who offered support, to the research professionals who offered assistance. Thanks in particular to the staffs of the Museum of the City of New York, the New-York Historical Society, and the New York Public Library.

Thanks to my sister, Jamie Broder, who provided free legal services along with free encouragement. And thanks to my parents, King and Mindie Broder, whose wisdom and support make every journey more promising and more worthwhile.

Special thanks to Rick Allen, my MacBook consultant, who is always there when I need him, which is recurrently. Thanks to friends who have helped in other ways, including Jim Downey, Gary Greenhill, Jeff Mangum, Ryan Ostrosky, Jen Poulsen, Hank Shaw, and Mary Shustack.

And devoted thanks to Patricia Greenhill, who along the way has contributed everything from blogging tutorials to a really comfortable chair. If not for her, you would now be reading some other book. And if not for her, I would know far less about patience, faith, and love.

Introduction

$\mathcal{I}$ was looking forward to sharing the story of the coffee shop with the airplane seats, especially since I had already gone to the trouble of writing it.

But you won't find it here. The coffee shop has been grounded, stranding thousands of passengers, along with my thousand-word write-up. The coffee shop was The Primeburger. It was almost fifty years old. It was also one of the places that inspired this book. Its prime features were its box seats with swiveling fake-walnut tray tables, which called to mind airline decor, if not oversize high chairs. With those seats, along with its space-age lights and white-jacketed waiters, The Primeburger did a matchless impression of 1965. And its history reached back to the forties, when it began as Hamburg Heaven, which, as irony would have it, is where it ended up.

When businesses are around for a long time, you never know how much longer they've got. Rents go up. Owners step down. Buildings get sold (ask The Primeburger). Haunts that you think of as permanent can vaporize in a flash. That's the punishment for writing a book about them. Also the reason.

I first thought of this project years ago, and it got steadily more manageable: Place after place that I would have written about shut down. I decided that I'd better start writing before the title *Vintage New York* was forced to refer to spots that had been around for more than a week.

So I visited the classic restaurants, shops, and nightspots of Manhattan, and I put several dozen of those places in one place. Of those, I spotlighted fifty. I wrote what each is like now and how it got that way. I did a really swell job on The Primeburger.

The places are old, but this isn't a book about old places. The places are historic, but this isn't a book about historic places. It's a book about old and historic places that take you back in time—places that can make you feel like you're back where they started. They range from a newsstand that serves egg creams to a cabaret that serves caviar; from a deli that gives you a ticket to a restaurant that gives you no menu. They include the home of the power lunch and the home of the hot-dog-and-papaya lunch. It's hard to imagine that there isn't something in here for everyone.

The spots range in age from just under 50 to over 150, but not every spot in Manhattan within that age range is here. There were rules. Foremost among them was that the place had to look the part. If it didn't take you to a specific era, it had to at least get you out of this one. It wasn't enough to be "established 1892," if the place making that claim looked more like it was established Thursday. It wasn't enough to bear the name of a famous New York destination, if the name was about the only remaining link to that destination.

I focused on places that you visit for fun, aware that fun is subjective. You can have fun at a hardware store; still, I did not include one. On the same principle, I omitted the likes of drug stores and butcher shops. Except for the exceptions. Choosing was not an exact science. But I chose comfortably sized spots, since there were enough to go around. There are no hotels, museums, theaters, department stores, skyscrapers, or monuments here. Those kinds of places all have plenty of books of their own. This one is for spots where a big crowd is always a small one.

In short, I chose places that some of us see as the heart of New York—the ones that created the city that's squeezing the likes of them out. When places like these close, people who always meant to visit them start grieving. I wrote this book to save you some grief. I didn't write it to proclaim my preference for a bygone city, though I just did. I wrote it to encourage people to enjoy what's left of that city. I also wrote it because there's more to enjoy at a place whose story you know, and all the places I've chosen have stories that are well worth knowing.

In telling the stories, I was determined to write the most accurate histories possible. I learned that in some cases, accurate histories are impossible. Legends passed down as facts often change with each telling and may not have been true to start with. I got as close as I could.

Similarly, I learned that there are multiple concepts of birth. In a culture that prizes youth, old joints somehow always want to be older. Many trace their start, for instance, to another business at the same location. Origin years can be tricky. I got as logical as I could.

I mention prices when they're extraordinary, meaning real low or real high. Otherwise, assume that everything costs more than you think. I mention celebrities occasionally, but all these places have served celebrities. Don't visit these spots to see a star. Visit them to be a star.

My original title for this project was *True New York*. I changed that not just because it was vague but because it was presumptuous. It suggested that the only "true" New York is the old one, which isn't true. Truth may be a matter of fact, but trueness is a matter of taste. "Vintage" was a better word. It refers to things that are old and good, and to things that are the best of what they represent. The places in this book are among the best of New York, old or new. And they represent discovery for anybody, visitor or resident.

They may end up victims of change. But then, they were products of change. For better and for worse, New York City becomes what reality makes it. I may not like what reality's making it now, but millions apparently do. And millions who come here for what's new also support what's old.

I must be grateful to them, because their support helped to make it possible for me to spend the better part of a year at these places.

And I must be grateful to The Primeburger, even if its departure made me have to write an extra story. I'm lucky it was just one.

ARGOSY BOOK STORE

116 E. 59TH ST. • NEW YORK, NY 10022

(212) 753-4455 • ARGOSYBOOKS.COM

A Real Page-Turner

If you want to get a good idea of what's inside the Argosy Book Store, just spend some time poking around outside the Argosy Book Store.

Outside the Argosy Book Store is a court called the arcade, which offers a sneak preview of what's beyond the doors. A recent preview featured an Audubon duck print, a signed Truman letter, a signed Gershwin check, an antique map of Flanders, and a table piled with three-dollar cookbooks. Argosy appears to be a sanctum of priceless treasures, but as the arcade reveals, it has something for anyone. It does indeed have treasures, and some of them cost thousands of dollars. And some of them cost tens of dollars. And some of them cost three dollars.

And some of them cost one dollar. The arcade also has bookshelves packed with nothing but one-dollar books. Like most bookstores, Argosy has too many books, so it sells some off cheap, to keep things in order, to give you a break, and to get the people outside inside.

If they go in, they won't regret it. Argosy is a retreat. It's calm, quiet, and soothing, which bookstores should be but often aren't. It looks like an old-time library, with its wooden tables and green lampshades. And it's packed with stuff that's as uncommon as the store itself.

The main floor is lined with antiquarian and out-of-print books on such civilized topics as art, music, poetry, and philosophy. On a balcony at the rear are handsome leather-bound sets of Shakespeare, Dickens, Shelley, Wordsworth, and Bernard Shaw. But beyond those shelves are bins packed with paper surprises, through which, if you were so inclined, you could spend a day poking. Your finds could range from a print of Edward Sackville, Fourth Earl of Dorset, to the original sheet music for "That Tumble Down Shack in Athlone."

All the things in those bins are $10, except for the ones that are $3, again proving that Argosy prices are not prohibitive. "There's something for absolutely everyone," says one of the owners, Naomi Hample. "It's fun just to look—to see what the next one's going to be."

More surprises are near the entrance, where there's a cart of more three-dollar books and bins of three-dollar end papers and antique book covers. And there's a collection of letters and photographs signed by personalities from Janet Leigh to Oliver Stone to Patty Duke.

Completing the floor is Select Reading, an earnest collection of, in Naomi's words, "things you meant to read one day but never did." Typical titles include *The Complete Works of O. Henry, The Complete Letters of Oscar Wilde, The Diary of Anne Frank,* and *The Most of George Burns.*

"That's my baby," Naomi says. "I'm very fussy about what I put in there. I don't want to pollute it. If I don't have something good, I'd rather leave a space." But then, that's more or less the store's philosophy, which becomes ever clearer as you climb ever higher.

On the second floor is the Gallery, filled with antique maps and prints, along with posters, newspapers, and occasional globes. The prints are filed by subject, as in children, fishing, and flowers; the maps are filed by region, as in India, Virginia, and Yonkers. Here, too, the search is seductive; this is a serious collection. People get sidetracked, says Laura Ten Eyck, the Gallery director. "Someone will come in to find a map of an obscure county in Illinois," she says, "and then they'll end up in the aardvark folder."

On the third through sixth floors are American history books, first editions, rare books, manuscripts, and a trove of framed autographs. Regarding the autographs, Naomi says, "My specialty is having no specialty. It's having everything, from movie stars to presidents to writers."

You are accompanied by elevator to the upper floors, but you can walk all by yourself down to the basement. There you can spend hours amid more aisles of books. The titles in the music section range from *The Beethoven Quartets* to *Merle Haggard's My House of Memories.*

Naomi seems as proud of those books as she is of the framed autographs. She may be as proud of the dollar books as she is of the antique maps. She clearly loves the store, which is understandable, since the store has always been part of the family.

Argosy was founded in 1925 by Louis Cohen, her father. He had two reasons for choosing the name, she says. "An argosy implies a treasure ship, and I think that's appropriate for the kind of store we are. And the second reason was that he wanted to be under the letter A in the phone book."

He opened the store on the stretch of Fourth Avenue that was known as Book Row and moved it to 59th Street in 1930. In 1953 he bought the building that it's in now, and in 1964 he moved the store there. Meanwhile, he and his wife, Ruth, who created the Gallery, had three daughters. All three went to work in the store. Along with Naomi, Adina Cohen and Judith Lowry still work there today. The daughters are three of the owners. Judith's son Ben Lowry is the fourth.

They all aim for accessibility, with attractions like the three-dollar book table (whose book subject changes every few weeks). But the place still scares some people off. And the place can do only so much about it: "We don't want to look off-putting," Naomi says, "but it is what it is."

ARON STREIT, INC.

148–154 RIVINGTON ST. • NEW YORK, NY 10002

(212) 475-7000 • STREITSMATZOS.COM

In No Time Flat

*T*here are lots of rabbis who can tell you that matzo is the unleavened bread that Jews traditionally eat at Passover. There's one rabbi who can tell you that Aron Streit, Inc., makes two and a half million boxes of it a year.

That would be Rabbi Mayer Kirshner, who can tell you this because he works at Aron Streit, Inc., as the matzo rabbi. And he will tell you this if you arrange to meet him at the factory, because, as the matzo rabbi, he is also the matzo tour guide.

Aron Streit, Inc., better known as Streit's Matzos, is the last major family-owned matzo baker in the US. It bakes matzos in its original factory, which dates back nearly a century. And while the factory's for making matzos, it's also for seeing matzos made.

You can do that in part without any rabbinical assistance. Just walk up to the building and look through the window bars. You can see matzos in scored sheets sliding out of a seventy-foot oven, and men called pickers breaking the sheets into squares and loading them into racks.

If you're lucky, a man will hand you a piece of hot matzo through the window. If you're not, you can ask the man to hand you a piece, and he probably will. It's a nice treat, especially on a cold day, since matzo is rarely served hot, and also since in New York things are rarely served free.

If you're luckier still, you might get the rest of the tour, in which you can see matzo dough rolled, flattened, cut, and perforated. And if you're not, you can make an appointment, which is well worth making, because a ninety-year-old matzo factory can't last forever.

On the tour, the rabbi will tell you that the factory was founded by Aron Streit, though in 1925 he had a different rabbi. He will tell you that the factory makes Passover matzo for six months a year and non-Passover matzo for the other six months a year. You may be surprised to learn that so much non-Passover matzo is made, and you may be just as surprised to learn that it comes in about fifteen flavors. You can now have your non-Passover matzo in varieties including Egg & Onion and Onion-Poppy Moonstrips.

In short, you will get the matzo education of a lifetime, which you should, since you may not come here more than once in your life. And you'll appreciate it, because you'll have learned not just about a factory but also about the family that made the factory.

Among the family members running it now is Aron Streit Yagoda, who is the great-grandson of Aron Streit. He likes his job. He's not sure whether his great-grandfather liked his job, but he's pretty sure that his great-grandfather would like that he likes his job.

In the late 1800s, Aron Streit was making matzo in Austria. He came to America, which gave him the opportunity to make matzo in New York. He did that at first with a Rabbi Weinberger, and about twenty years later opened his own factory. He clearly built it to last at least a century. He ran the factory with his sons, Irving and Jack. When he died, in 1937, Irving and Jack took over. Irving was the president until he died, in 1980. Then Jack became the president. But Streit's has never put much stock in titles.

Jack ran the factory till he died, in 1998. It was then run by Aron Yagoda (his grandson) and Mel Gross (Irving's grandson) till Mel died. It is now run by Aron, Alan Adler (Irving's other grandson), and Aaron Gross (Irving's great-grandson). Jack's daughter Arlyne—Aron's mother—also worked at the factory. So did Irving's daughter Muriel Fisher. It all attests to what family devotion can do for a product that was, at least in its origin, essentially a mistake.

Matzo is known as the bread that didn't have time to rise when Jews were fleeing slavery in Egypt, around 3,500 years ago. It's now a symbol of liberation, and as such it's eaten throughout Passover to remind Jews that freedom is more important than wealth.

In contrast to the slaves, Streit's makes its matzo on purpose. It also makes it in a more modern way, though not that much more modern. Its ancient machines blend flour and water, flatten and cut the dough, send the dough sheets into the ovens, and seal the baked squares into boxes. It's all done under the watch of Rabbi Kirshner, who patrols the five floors, making sure everything is done according to the laws of kosher. You can't update kosher. But you can update product lines. That's why the factory store has non-factory products like Streit's Chow Mein Noodles.

There are now dozens of Streit's products, but the bread and butter is still matzo. Maybe that's why some customers get so serious about it. "People come in with ideas," Aron says. "They say, 'I have an idea for round matzo' or 'Put a hole in it, and make it look like a bagel.'"

He listens politely. Usually. He likes to be a good neighbor, regardless of the past century's changes in the neighborhood. "Kids pass by here coming home from school, they put their hands in the window and get free matzo. And it's not Jewish kids."

"It's a free cracker," he says, "an afternoon snack for kids who don't have any money in their pocket. I get a kick out of it."

"If one of us is here and we're in a good mood, we'll take you on a tour," he adds. "We want to be like a hip company. We want to be cool."

The Old Stomping Ground

*I*t's partly because they love to play, partly because they play for love, and partly because, against the odds, they keep showing up. But it's mostly because they put on a good show. They'd have to, to keep the show running for 2,600 weeks.

They are the Grove Street Stompers, and they have a steady gig. They play every Monday night at Arthur's Tavern in the West Village. As the math reveals, to have played on more than 2,600 Mondays, they would have to have been playing for fifty years. Which they have.

The band's leader knows they have, since he is not only their leader but also their founder, as well as their piano player. He is Bill Dunham, and he was there in 1962 when the Stompers played Arthur's for the first time. He figures they've set a record.

The Stompers play three sets, from seven o'clock until ten o'clock. They play Dixieland, which was considered quaint thirty years before they started. They end each set, every night, with "Mood Indigo." That makes 7,800 "Mood Indigos." They play "Up a Lazy River" and "Rose of Washington Square" and "Let Me Call You Sweetheart" and "I'll See You in My Dreams." They play "The Best Things in Life Are Free," which proves to be true, since their show is free, if you don't count the two-drink minimum.

They play on piano, clarinet, trombone, trumpet, string bass, and drums, and they'll add a piece if one of the substitute Stompers shows up. They are a tribute to, above all, improbability, which makes them a perfect match for their venue.

Arthur's is not the Café Carlyle, where Woody Allen plays on Monday nights. It is a dive, which can be charming as long as the lights are low. It has an old wooden bar with thirteen stools, a wall with ten tables and twenty chairs, and a path that leads to a stage that can't hold much more than six Stompers.

On the wall are "Happy Halloween" banners and a glittery Easter Bunny; at the bar are Christmas stockings and a Valentine's Day heart. Above are fake-pine garlands, balloons, and a rainbow of colored lights. Arthur's accommodates you. Whatever you're celebrating, it's celebrating.

Arthur's has other regulars, who appear on other nights, including a bluesy belter named Sweet Georgia Brown. But none can touch the Stompers in the category of commitment. Their few absences have had excuses on the order of the funeral of John F. Kennedy.

Bill first played Arthur's in the fifties, with a group he called the Village Six. He chose a career in business, but that's no substitute for the piano. He formed the Stompers with a graphic designer named Jimmy Gribbon on cornet, and five others, including an airline captain and a bulldozer salesman. The seventh man was on banjo; he died a few years later. Bill decided to leave the lineup at six. Stompers have come and gone, but Bill figures that there have been only about two dozen in all, not counting substitutes, of which he always stocks six per instrument.

The second-longest-running member of the group is Peter Ballance, by day a stockbroker, who has been the Stompers' trombonist for about forty years. But the only original member is Bill. "All the others had the good sense to die off," he says. "I'm the only one left."

"I fired three people over the years," he adds, "including a beloved drummer who was getting older and wasn't drumming right. And I fired two guys for getting drunk on the stand, including a bass player who had the remarkable ability of being passed out and still playing bass."

Bill refers to himself as an amateur, but in contrast to the early days, he considers all the other members professionals. In 2012, for their golden anniversary, the Stompers recorded a CD—their third album—live at Arthur's, of course.

Arthur's is said to have opened in 1937. No one seems to have any recollection of Arthur. The rusted neon sign outside says ARTHUR'S STEAKS CHOPS. But in fifty years, Bill says, he's never seen a steak or a chop, though for a while he saw a popcorn machine.

Whatever the tavern served, it was owned for decades by the Maisano family, members of which kept it into the eighties. Then Danny Bensusan, who had loved the place, bought the bar and its building. A couple of years earlier, he had founded the Blue Note jazz club.

In its early days, Danny says, Arthur's was favored by swells. Men wore tuxedos. Naturally, legends abound. One has it that the young Charlie Parker once arrived there by taxi but couldn't pay the fare. He got it from Vinnie Maisano, then played sax to work it off.

Obviously, the Maisanos knew how to cut a deal. Any Grove Street Stomper who's rich didn't get that way at Arthur's. In half a century, Bill says, they've had two raises, which have brought them up to $30 apiece per night, plus tips. Plus an extra $5 for the leader.

"If I'd been real pushy about getting more money from the Maisanos," Bill says, "they would've kicked us out of there." But there has been the occasional windfall.

"A guy came in once on St. Patrick's Day, well into his cups. He said, 'Can you play an Irish tune?' I said, 'No, we don't know any Irish tunes.' Bingo! He slapped fifty bucks on the piano. We broke into ['The Irish Washerwoman']. He slapped another fifty, and we played 'Irish Eyes.' So we made a quick hundred bucks."

Mangia Like a King

*I*f you can remember when one dressed to go to a restaurant, Barbetta will probably make you feel like you should have dressed. If you can't remember when one dressed to go to a restaurant, Barbetta will probably still make you feel like you should have dressed.

The main dining room at Barbetta heightens your self-awareness. It has no dress code, yet it seems to give you the once-over. It silently asks, "Is that really how you want to be dressed to be in a palace?" It has the right, for the room itself is dressed to be in a palace.

It re-creates eighteenth-century Piemonte, Italy, in a grand space with palatial chairs and sconces and a chandelier that actually is from a palace. It invites you to imagine what royal living was like in Italy, and it invites you to recall what elegant dining was like in New York. It is billed as the oldest restaurant in the city that's still owned by its founding family, but it is not quite the restaurant that its founder created. It was opened as a fine restaurant by Sebastiano Maioglio in 1906. It was turned into an opulent restaurant by his daughter in 1962. Its menu, which gives the year in which every selection was first served, lists a few selections from both of those years. They help to tell the story of a daughter who devoted herself to turning something that her father thought of into something that he never dreamed of.

"My father had sold the restaurant when I was in college," says Laura Maioglio. "When I heard of it, I was shocked. I said, 'Why have you done this? Why don't you want to keep it in the family?' He looked at me, and he just said, 'It's not for you.'"

It was a reasonable thing to say to a girl who had just earned a degree in art history from Bryn Mawr and who had never worked in a restaurant. Still, she says, "I pleaded with him and even started to shed tears." Her explanation today: "I'm sentimental to the point that it's a fault."

So it's her fault that her father relented and backed out of the deal, and that his restaurant has survived for another half century. It's her fault that it's now apparently the oldest Italian restaurant in the city and that it was arguably the first elegant Italian restaurant in the city.

From Sebastiano's Barbetta you can still order things like minestrone giardiniera, and risotto alla Piemontese with wild porcini mushrooms. From Laura's Barbetta, you can get later Piemontese dishes like bue al barolo, and quail's nest of fonduta with quail eggs. They somehow all fit together, which could seem like chance. But the Maioglios have rarely taken chances on chance.

Sebastiano came here from Piemonte determined to succeed. "He felt he was a burden to his family," Laura says. "He felt he had to leave." He opened a place designed to be accessible and affordable. He gave it an accessible name: Maioglio Brothers Restaurant. The brother was Vincenzo, who arrived soon after Sebastiano. He helped run the place till he died, in 1926. In tribute to him, Sebastiano rechristened the restaurant with Vincenzo's nickname, Barbetta, which means "little beard."

When Sebastiano died, Laura embarked on a tribute of her own. She had a vision of Piemontese ambience that transcended the food. She traveled Europe to collect the furnishings that would help her to realize it. The art history degree came in handy after all. She bought Piemontese antiques, and the ones that she couldn't find she arranged to have expertly reproduced. She had the 180 dining chairs copied from a palatial original. She bargained for two years to get the main chandelier out of a palace bedroom.

"I didn't have the idea to make it upscale," she says. "But once I finished the interior, it was upscale." And once the interior was upscale, "the menu and the service had to match. So I went around the city and took notes at upscale restaurants."

The year after she reopened, she added a lush dining garden, which set the standard for the city restaurant gardens that have followed. Since then, she has added other rooms spanning the four Victorian town houses that Sebastiano had had the foresight to snap up.

She has indeed attracted royalty—at least American royalty, meaning guests from Elizabeth Taylor to the Clintons. She has won awards for her food and her wine. In 1976 she married Dr. Günter Blobel, who won the 1999 Nobel Prize in Medicine. She has also compiled a long list of restaurant firsts, of whose veracity she is characteristically confident. Under Sebastiano, for instance, Barbetta was the first to serve risotto, polenta, and wild porcini mushrooms (which were picked by Sebastiano himself). Under her watch, she says, Barbetta was the first to serve, among other things, white truffles, sun-dried tomatoes, panna cotta, and decaf espresso. And it was the first to discourage smoking by filling its matchboxes with chocolate mints instead of with matches.

Most important, though, Barbetta was the first restaurant to give meaningful employment to Piera Maioglio—Laura's mother. When Laura took over, she asked her mother to come help her, she says. "She loved the job. She loved the public. That was the best twenty years of her life."

Prepare to Be Appetized

You could go to one of those museums that have fake general stores, or you could go to Barney Greengrass and be in a real general store. But only at Barney Greengrass could you get Nova Scotia salmon scrambled with eggs and onions, not to mention pickled herring in cream sauce.

Barney Greengrass is what's known as an appetizing store, which is a Jewish specialty food store where the specialty is fish—specifically smoked and cured fish, particularly sturgeon, salmon, whitefish, and sable, prepared so as to be appetizing. If you're appetized by fish.

But it has the look of a general store because it opened in 1929 and mostly stayed there, except for its prices and its presiding Greengrass. Its unlikely marriage of downscale decor and upscale delicacies has made it among the most treasured spots on the Upper West Side. Within walls painted thirties green it displays its wares on shelves and in cases of art deco white-and-black porcelain enamel. The cases credit themselves to "Royal Store Fixture Co./Max Rosen/New York City." If Max were around today, other food stores might be as royal.

Amid the faded grandeur, devotees pick up sackfuls of their favorites or stay and feast at white Formica-topped tables with gray-sparkle vinyl chairs. Then again, if they prefer modern times, they can sit in the adjacent dining room, which will whisk them from 1929 to 1958.

You could go to one of those joints decorated with fake fifties wallpaper, or you could go to Barney Greengrass and see real fifties wallpaper. But only at Barney Greengrass—at least more than likely only here—will the fifties wallpaper be beige and have scenes of old New Orleans.

With that backdrop, you can sit at the wood-grain Formica-topped tables, or perhaps on the forest-green padded-vinyl bench or chairs amid wood-grain Formica wainscoting. Some see it as preservation; others see it as neglect. But most love it. And most come back. Barney Greengrass is something to count on.

"We're a comfortable shoe," says Gary, the presiding Greengrass, in one of his favorite store characterizations. "Old world, old flavor—that's what we're about. People who haven't been here in twenty years come in and say, 'I'm glad you haven't touched anything.'"

Gary is the grandson of Barney, who founded the store in Harlem in 1908 and moved it to its current home in 1929. Tradition has it that the state senator James Frawley dubbed Barney "The Sturgeon King," and the sobriquet stuck. It follows the store's name to this day.

Barney was succeeded by his son Marvin, known as Moe, who became known for impulsively entertaining the customers with card tricks. On one side of a store column hangs a framed photo of Moe with Danny Kaye. On another side hangs a framed portrait of Barney, beneath an amberjack caught by Gary. Gary apprenticed with Moe, as Moe had apprenticed with Barney. He took over in the eighties, after rejecting broadcast journalism. His older brother, Barney, despite his name, makes his living on Wall Street. He chose stocks over lox, but Gary says he doesn't regret picking lox.

Barney's has enticed, besides Danny Kaye, luminaries from Franklin Roosevelt to Irving Berlin to Groucho Marx to Marilyn Monroe. But the store depends on the fans who line up—especially on weekends—for what it does best, which the menu makes reasonably clear. The first three choices listed under Appetizers are: sturgeon; Nova Scotia salmon; and sturgeon and Nova Scotia salmon. The first three sandwich specialties are: sturgeon;

Nova Scotia salmon; and sturgeon and Nova Scotia salmon. The first three choices under Eggs & Omelettes are: eggs with side of sturgeon; eggs with side of Nova Scotia salmon; and eggs with side of sturgeon and Nova Scotia salmon.

Or you could get a cream cheese and jelly sandwich. But it won't tell you why fans line up to spend twenty bucks on a specialty.

Lines notwithstanding, the biggest day of the year for Barney Greengrass is the day on which many Jews refrain from eating. It's Yom Kippur, the Day of Atonement. It calls for penance, including fasting. But when the fast is over, the meal to break it is sent to hundreds of homes by Barney's.

"On the week before Yom Kippur I'm here every night till twelve or one in the morning," Gary says. On the day before the holiday starts, he's back at seven or eight in the morning and stays till 5:30 on Yom Kippur Eve. He goes home, cleans up, and heads for temple: "I fall asleep standing in the synagogue."

Barney's also caters and sells by mail order all year long. And on those general-store shelves it stocks specialty-store foods. They include boxes of matzos, jars of capers, and cans of hearts of palm, along with appetizing store requisites like dried fruits and halvah.

In the nineties Gary opened a second Barney's, in Beverly Hills. It's on the fifth floor of the previously unrelated Barneys New York. But he has declined to open at other locations, including Grand Central Terminal. One store is enough, he seems to say. Two are more than enough.

Which leaves one compelling question about Barney Greengrass history: Why did the place buy wallpaper with scenes of old New Orleans? It is definitely New Orleans. And Gary credibly explains it. "It's from the late fifties," he says. "It was probably on sale that week."

BIG NICK'S
BURGER JOINT & PIZZA JOINT

2175 BROADWAY • NEW YORK, NY 10024

(212) 362-9238 • BIGNICKSNYC.COM

He Wrote the Book

*I*f you go to Big Nick's to eat, make sure you leave time to read. The menu has twenty-eight pages. The walls have six dozen signs. Just remember that it's Big Nick's Burger Joint & Pizza Joint, which ought to give you direction, though burgers and pizza alone take up seven of the pages.

Big Nick's is the forerunner of the Facebook wall—a place splattered with information, none of which you're sure you need. But this is amusing information. This is appetizing information. This guides you to making your best possible selection of joint food.

If you want a burger, your choices include not only the Aloha Burger (with pineapple and ham) and the Phila Burger (with cream cheese and olive), but also the Stuffed Gorgonzola Burger, the Stuffed Burger Florentine, and the Stuffed Western Burger with peppers, onions, and ham. Those are among the forty-three burgers in The Hamburger Experience, which is separate from the Specialty Burgers experience, which has seventeen more. There's a Big Nick Burger in a Pocket; there's a Big Nick Burger Club; there's a Burger Kebab, featuring a Big Nick Grecian Burger Croquette. Above all, there's the Sumo Burger, which is a pound as well as a bargain: "Twice the size of a Big Nick but not twice the price."

As for pizza, the slices come in, among others, regular, white, pan, Sicilian, tofu, stuffed, fricassee, and Big Nick Special (which has hamburger). The pies include Chicken Teriyaki, Sloppy Joe, Gyromania, Shrimp Piraeus, and the Big Nick Special (which has hamburger).

The rest of the menu covers everything from kofta kebabs to quesadillas, omitting virtually no foods that you've heard of and few that you haven't. You wonder where Nick keeps it all, since in either of the two joints, there's barely enough elbow room to make it to a table.

It's cozy. It's a dive. But Nick takes that as a compliment. The menu proudly posts quotes that call it not only a dive but a dump. As a Yelp comment puts it: "This isn't a date spot, nor is it a place you should bring anyone you'd want to impress professionally." That's debatable. But it makes a point.

Big Nick doesn't run a tearoom. He runs more of a truck stop. He doesn't offer sophistication; he offers satisfaction. "Big Nick Cares," says his heart on the menu cover, next to a quote from his mouth: "I don't compromise with quantity or quality—and always a reasonable price!"

Demetrios Niko Imirziades arrived in New York from Athens in 1961 as "an innocent Greek" of twenty. On the neighborhood menu, he recalls, were junkies, hookers, and pimps. "I didn't know where I was," he says. So he took a coffee-shop job washing dishes.

Inspired by his mother's cooking, he went to restaurant school in New York City, while rising at the coffee shop from dishwasher to cook to partner. He moved on to the nearby coffee shop that would become Big Nick's. In 1964 he bought it. He called it The Burger Joint. The Burger Joint did well, so he opened other joints. Over the years, he figures, he's opened a total of fifteen. At his peak, he was running six at once. They had names like Burger Joint Too, Burger Joint Also, and perhaps most memorably, The Burger Biter.

But the flagship was always The Burger Joint, whose fame grew after it introduced the half-pound Big Nick in response to the Big Mac. Since Nick was, in fact, big, having once thrown the discus, in 1976 he renamed his place Big Nick's.

Soon after, he added his Pizza Joint, and then opened more of those. But eventually he sold off all but his flagship joints. There's still a Big Nick's Burger Joint & Pizza Joint Too on 71st Street and Columbus, which doesn't seem to mind if you think that it's still owned by Big Nick.

Still influenced by the meals of his boyhood, Nick opened Niko's Mediterranean Grill & Bistro in the early nineties, a couple of doors down from Big Nick's. It, too, had burgers and pizzas, but nowhere near as many. The menu was noticeably refined. It had only twenty pages.

In 2011, though, Nick also gave up Niko's, for which his customers roundly admonished him. "They were thinking only 'me, me, me, me, me,'" he says. "Not that I serviced them for twenty years." Still, he recognized the compliment.

He gave the customers a consolation prize in 2012, when he celebrated Big Nick's fiftieth anniversary, whether or not it was. For one day, he sold food at the joints at 1962 prices. People lined up to buy hamburgers for sixty cents, his most reasonable price yet.

He's not sure how much longer he'll be able to run his joints, especially in a city of brutally rising rents. For now he plans to stay put. But the joint life isn't easy: "There are Three Brothers restaurants. There are Four Brothers restaurants. I'm a One Brother restaurant."

CAFÉ CARLYLE

35 E. 76TH ST. • NEW YORK, NY 10021

(212) 744-1600 • ROSEWOODHOTELS.COM

It's the Top

Jn the cabaret that's the quintessence of Manhattan sophistication, tonight's sophisticated star takes the stage strumming a ukulele. There is silence. "It's OK to laugh," the star says. "I'd be laughing if I were you." There is laughter. The star adds: "It's not something you're likely to see every day."

Yes, at the Café Carlyle you sometimes wait for permission to laugh. You're aware that if you're the only one laughing, everyone else will know it. But it's worth a little caution to have a New York night out in the boîte of the rich and famous, with the accent on the rich.

The Carlyle is the club with the musical-urchin murals and the beluga caviar at $285 an ounce. It's also the club where the performers sing as if they're in their living rooms, and as if you belong there with them.

The club began in the fifties, but its magic began in the sixties, when it brought in a rising singer and pianist named Bobby Short. The club and the singer instinctively underscored each other's elegance. In his four decades there, Bobby Short made the Carlyle what it is today.

It's a nightclub with a cover of around $100—except on Mondays, when Woody Allen appears and it's $135. But it's also a nightclub that reminds you of what at least some nightclubs were like before distracting devices, distracting music, and distracting pants.

The ukuleleist was Andrea Marcovicci, who was making her Carlyle debut, which is not to say that she hadn't made other debuts. She sang for twenty-five years in the Oak Room at the Algonquin Hotel. But true to the times, the Oak Room closed, so she scaled the cabaret peak.

"I love it," she said after the show, as she held court in the lobby. "It's so graceful. It's so elegant. It's a whole Fred Astaire experience. It's a magnificently elegant place to be." The Café Carlyle gets described as elegant a lot.

Marcovicci opened with "It's Only a Paper Moon," and the ukulele was, to say the least, unexpected. Still, the Carlyle is not austere. It wants you to have fun. The murals include a painting of a trained seal on a red ball, wearing a giant pearl necklace and a tiny tutu.

No doubt for fun, Moses Ginsberg built the hotel that would house the cafe. His daughter named it for the writer Thomas Carlyle. It opened in 1930 and would become the New York place to stay after President John F. Kennedy made it his White House in the city. In 1955 the hotel's second owner, Robert Dowling, "had it in his mind to create the ultimate Upper East Side supper club," writes Nick Foulkes in *The Carlyle.* Dowling set the tone with the fanciful murals that endure to this day, painted by the Hungarian artist Marcel Vertès.

He further set the tone with a grand piano, first played by a Hungarian composer and pianist named George Feyer. "Distinguished, soigné, and elegant in a dinner jacket," Foulkes writes, "Feyer struck exactly the right note for The Carlyle." It was a good start. And Feyer had a good run. He played at the Carlyle for thirteen years. In 1968 he took a vacation, and Bobby Short filled in. He had also had a good run. He played at the Carlyle for thirty-six years. He first played as a twelve-year-old in Danville, Illinois. And early on he took to the music that he would bring to the cafe.

"I acquired this penchant for the songs that I sang in my teens—for Porter, the Gershwins, Rodgers and Hart," he told me in an interview in 1991. "It didn't take me long to realize they were the cream of the crop, and I put forth my best efforts to do justice to their material."

He had made his Manhattan debut in 1945, at the storied Blue Angel. He was not a hit. "But I had tasted the glamour of New York," he said. So he worked on his act. And evidently he improved, because the Carlyle hired him at the start for eight months a year.

It was a lucky time to be hired to sing Porter and Gershwin, he said: "Performers who I'd known for years couldn't get a job. Careers were being ruined by the day because people didn't want to hear anything but rock 'n' roll." Maybe lots of people. But not all people.

Short was almost instantly the talk of the town. The talk intensified when he starred in a TV commercial for Charlie perfume. It steeped the nation in the Carlyle image of a tony New York night out, and incidentally helped to make Charlie the best-selling perfume in the world.

In time Short cut back to six months a year, and then to four, but his show increasingly became a destination. He died in 2005. The Carlyle lobby has a Bobby Short portrait, its street corner is Bobby Short Place, and its cafe menu offers Bobby Short's Chicken Hash.

Carrying on at the cafe, along with Marcovicci, are stars including Steve Tyrell and Judy Collins. On Mondays Woody Allen plays with the Eddy Davis New Orleans Jazz Band. (It was at Michael's Pub that he was playing when he won his Oscar for *Annie Hall*.)

Allen, who's put just about every Manhattan landmark into his movies, accordingly put Bobby Short into *Hannah and Her Sisters*. In a way, when you go to the Carlyle, you're still going because of Short. And yet Short was prone to feel as if he'd never quite made it.

At times, he told me, he wished he'd become more famous. But he always knew he'd achieved a goal shared by many—including him. In 1956, he said, he spent a night out at the Café Carlyle: "I thought, 'This is a marvelous room. I must work here one of these days.'"

CAFFÈ REGGIO

119 MACDOUGAL ST. • NEW YORK, NY 10012

(212) 475-9557 • CAFFEREGGIO.COM

Feel the Beats

*I*f you like coffee but not Starbucks, chances are you'll like Caffè Reggio, if you can forget that Caffè Reggio is kind of responsible for Starbucks. After all, it didn't mean to be. But the caffè couldn't be everywhere, and Starbucks, as its twenty thousand stores suggest, could. In any case, whether you love or hate the world's biggest coffeehouse chain, you can still try the place that beat it to the pot by forty-four years.

Reggio is the mythic Village hangout that's not a myth: It would look like it did eighty years ago if it weren't for the customers. They've changed styles, but the caffè hasn't; it's still a cluttered jumble of marble-topped tables and iron-backed chairs amid a cluttered jumble of antediluvian relics.

The central relic is the retired 1902 Italian espresso machine, displayed in its chrome-and-brass glory like a mechanized trophy. And it is a trophy. The caffè claims to have used it to make the first cappuccino in America, and if that doesn't make it kind of responsible for Starbucks, nothing does.

The machine is joined, as the menu puts it, by "over eighty separate works of art . . . some of which date back to the Italian Renaissance period." They include paintings, busts, plates, clocks, statues, and stained-glass windows, which you think ought to be in a museum until you realize that they are. The works include what's identified as a School of Caravaggio painting and a bench bearing the family crest of Lorenzo de' Medici. Yet for all their centuries, these pieces conjure up less history than the collective jumble, which for decades has been a vantage point for changing times in New York.

Vintage Spots: Greenwich Village

ARTURO'S: EST. 1957

If you like your pizza topped with jazz, this is your pizzeria: It has live jazz every night of the week. The coal-oven pie is the biggest star, but reportedly the founder needed entertainment: "My father was trapped here," says his son, "and he made it as much fun as he could for himself."

106 W. Houston St.; (212) 677-3820

BLEECKER BOB'S GOLDEN OLDIES: EST. 1967

A new invention called the CD has encroached, but this still feels like a record store, probably because it's still crammed with records. It began as Village Oldies and is now in danger of ending, but the management had faith that it could make it to publication day.

118 W. Third St.; (212) 475-9677; bleecker-bobs.blogspot.com

GENE'S RESTAURANT: EST. 1919

An old Gene's postcard says "Established 1923," but this place has never cared what year it is. It's just a nice Italian restaurant with nice Italian food. There are paintings and mirrors and wrought-iron bars, and your waiter wears a jacket, even if you don't.

73 W. 11th St.; (212) 675-2048; genesnyc.com

RAFFETTO'S FRESH PASTA: EST. 1906

You'll want to eat when you take your first sniff, which is a problem, since this isn't a restaurant. But you can buy homemade pastas and sauces and the prepared meals you're sniffing, and you can see the pasta getting guillotined on the 1917 noodle-cutter.

144 W. Houston St.; (212) 777-1261; raffettospasta.com

Reggio has been credited with introducing to this country not only cappuccino but also the very idea of a modern coffeehouse. In a 1976 book called *Folk Music: More Than a Song,* Kristin Baggelaar and Donald Milton hand the credit to Reggio's founder, Domenico Parisi. "His imported espresso machine," they write, "was a novelty which lured customers to gather, play checkers, and chat in a warm and friendly atmosphere; consequently the Reggio became a prototype for coffeehouses that were to follow." When they wrote that, Starbucks was five years old.

Reggio has long been a home to artists, and it's often mentioned as a favorite of Beat writers, notably Kerouac. It figures in a folk-music book because it was among the spots to welcome the rising stars of folk and rock in the storied Village of the sixties.

"A lot of famous people used to come over," says Fabrizio Prim Cavallacci, the current owner of Reggio and the son of the previous owner. "Bob Dylan would come in and put five dollars on the table and pay for the entire floor, 'cause he had probably made twenty dollars the night before."

Fabrizio agrees that Domenico Parisi helped make nights like that possible because, apparently, the guy was born for business.

"It was a barber shop," Fabrizio says of Domenico's place in the twenties. "He was shaving people at ten cents a shot. After a while, the Italians were asking if he had coffee. He said, 'I'll make you some coffee.' So he sold coffee at ten cents a shot.

"He saw that it takes twenty-five to thirty-five minutes to give a shave, and it takes two seconds to make a coffee. He said, 'I'll stop shaving people, and I'll start selling coffee.' He bought this big, huge espresso machine. The guy wasn't that stupid." He switched from barber to barista in 1927.

The machine is said to have been built for a world's fair in Italy and to have cost Domenico $1,000, his life's savings. According to a story in the *New York Herald Tribune,* he let no one else touch the machine, and thus, if he got sick, he closed up the caffè.

But as *Folk Music* says, the machine made the shop, which is why the shop was around when Niso and Hilda Cavallacci were ready for it. The family came here in the fifties, and Niso and his brother started a marble factory. While they worked, Hilda stayed at home and got bored.

"They came to the Village one day and saw this tiny place," Fabrizio says. "They liked the artworks that were in it. They liked the furniture." They asked Domenico if he'd sell. He said sure—for $10,000. "My father said, 'You must be out of your mind.'"

But Domenico, still good with numbers, wasn't lowering this one. "He said, 'You come see what kind of sales we have and see if the place is worth it.' And the place was worth it." So Niso bought it in 1956, mostly for Hilda, who ended up with a cure for boredom.

"My mother used to be the only waitress, and she served the people all by herself," Fabrizio says. "She would open up around eleven o'clock and be on her own till six or seven o'clock. She used to make twenty to twenty-five dollars in tips and used that money to raise a family."

Fabrizio worked in the shop as a boy and took over in his teens. "Sometimes you just have to grow up," he reflects. It was the seventies, which was not the best time in the life of Reggio, and not the best time in the life of the city. "It was dangerous," he recalls. "There was a lot of drugs, a lot of prostitution, you name it. It was not for a kid. Then NYU came in and cleaned up the area, and after that business started dropping. People are attracted to crime."

Niso could have bought his building in 1956 for $20,000. He didn't. So Fabrizio bought it in 1982 for $2 million. But that still turned out to be a bargain, and it also turned out to be the key to the survival of Reggio in a Starbucks world.

He's glad of that, because he's come to appreciate the caffè's past, even if that past was before his past. He likes the Dylan story. But he points out that it didn't make Dylan so much of a sport. "Cappuccino was thirty-five cents then," he says. "Ten cappuccinos were three-fifty."

Face the Big Choices

I told Sandy Levine that people say his restaurant is a tourist trap. Sandy pulled me by the arm through the restaurant, vowing to prove them right.

Surprisingly, he failed in his first attempt. "Where are you from?" he asked a woman. "New York," she said. "New York?" he barked. "What the hell ya doin' here? You got lost?" But after that he made good on the vow, as we hit table after table and got responses like Flagstaff, Pittsburgh, Syracuse, Mexico City, and Argentina.

Sandy is the retired manager of the Carnegie Delicatessen, one of the New York landmarks that make their living off people other than New Yorkers. In 2012 it turned seventy-five, which Sandy says it might not have if it hadn't become a tourist trap sometime after it turned fifty.

Its major attraction is a meat sandwich that, in weight and height, equals your last four combined. "A New Yorker's not gonna come in here and spend seventeen dollars on a sandwich," Sandy says. "We could make it smaller, but in business you have to be different. It's different. It's challenging."

The challenge is happily taken up daily by hundreds of city visitors eager to get their hands on a famous one-pound pile of pastrami. They get a New York meal to text home about, leftovers for a snack, and, occasionally, a visit from a staffer asking if they've had enough to eat.

The $17, incidentally, can be just a starting point. That buys a single-meat sandwich that's about five inches tall. But you can instead choose a

Gargantuan Combo for $25, bumping the meat to a pound and a half and the height to eight inches.

Unlike the late Stage Delicatessen, the Carnegie doesn't name most sandwiches for celebrities. But there's a Woody Allen, because the Carnegie was in Allen's *Broadway Danny Rose*. It has "lotsa corned beef plus lotsa pastrami," though every sandwich here has lotsa something.

Whatever you have lotsa, you get to eat it in either the original dining room or in the room added in 1991, which looks as old as the old room. In the old room you can imagine yourself eating beside a tableful of comedians, the way it was in the movie, which is the way it really was.

And in either room you can enjoy the walls, which in Jewish deli tradition are obscured by hundreds of framed photos of famous customers. Among the framed are Jon Stewart, Britney Spears, Kenny Rogers, Pat Sajak, Cal Ripken Jr., and Miss America 2008.

As for the menu, it offers traditions from chicken soup and chopped liver, to knishes and blintzes, to cheesecake and chocolate egg creams. But the Carnegie has long been known for size, which, as history suggests, may have been its destiny from the start.

That was in 1937, when a couple named Izzie and Ida Orgel opened it at the location it occupies to this day. Back then it had just forty seats and was just one of hundreds of Jewish delis. But the Orgels named it after Carnegie Hall. Already they were thinking big.

They sold it to Max Hudes in 1942, around the time that the Stage moved to the Carnegie's block. The Stage had also opened in 1937 and was run by Max Asnas. "Carnegie Max" did his best to compete for thirty-four years, but the Stage remained the bigger star.

That would change in 1976, when the Carnegie Deli began its new life under Leo Steiner and Milton Parker. Steiner, a seasoned deli man, decided to cure his own meats in the basement. Three years later that decision would change the course of deli history.

Vintage Spots: Midtown West

Jean's Silversmiths: est. 1910

It gleams with the likes of silver pitchers, bowls, trays, and tea sets, along with one of the biggest collections of American sterling flatware. Originally a curiosity shop, it was renamed by Armand Guior after he saw a play about a celebrated silver collector named Jean Valjean.

16 W. 45th St.; (212) 575-0723; jeanssilversmiths.com

Oyster Bar: est. 1959

This is not the century-old Oyster Bar in Grand Central Terminal. It's the half-century-old Oyster Bar in the theater district. They're not related. But unlike the other one, this Oyster Bar has neon signs, an ocean mural, shells on the ceiling, and a fake ship with a fake captain.

842 Seventh Ave.; (212) 586-6525; nyoysters.com

Patsy's Italian Restaurant: est. 1944

In seven decades, it's had three chefs, and one of them was Patsy. And the other two have been Patsy's son and grandson. That's one of the reasons the place has been favored by stars, chief among them the Chairman, Frank Sinatra, who's still here as a bronze statue.

236 W. 56th St.; (212) 247-3491; patsys.com

In 1979 the *New York Times* food writer Mimi Sheraton wrote a giant story about pastrami and corned beef. She named the Carnegie one of the three best places (and the only one in Midtown) to get it. Before the story ran, she was kind enough to warn Steiner to brace himself.

On the morning the story came out, lines formed at the Carnegie. Though he'd doubled his stock, Steiner ran out of pastrami by three o'clock. Milton Parker, in his Carnegie memoir, *How to Feed Friends and Influence People,* wrote: "Everything good that happened afterward to the Carnegie Deli can be traced to this generous article."

Actually, to the article and to Steiner, who brought not only his hand-curing and his recipes, but also his perfectly cast self. Steiner cracked wise, handed out samples, created the comedians' table, and convinced his more pragmatic partner that a sandwich was meant to be big.

Stars loved Steiner's Carnegie—and they knew that they were stars when they were presented with one of his ceremonial linen napkins. Steiner was to the deli born. In Parker's book, he's quoted as responding to requests for lean pastrami with: "If you want lean pastrami, order the turkey breast."

Steiner died in 1987, at which time Parker emerged from the background and proved himself a worthy if reluctant deli lama. In the spirit of his partner, he enlarged the sandwiches by two more inches. Parker oversaw the transition from New Yorker haunt to tourist attraction.

He also oversaw some failure. He opened Carnegies elsewhere that tanked. (Today there's one in Las Vegas and another in Bethlehem, Pennsylvania.) But he opened a commissary in New Jersey, which now does the curing and sends Carnegie products to retailers and distributors across the country.

Milton Parker died in 2009. Since then the deli's been run by his daughter Marian Harper Levine. In 1993 Sandy left the apparel industry to work for Parker. He got business cards that said "Sandy Levine/MBD." The letters stood for "Married Boss's Daughter."

At the end of 2012, Sandy stepped down, and the Stage bowed out. But Marian says that no one has to worry about the Carnegie. "We own the building," she says. "We want the Carnegie to be here another seventy-five years. There's nothing like a good corned beef, and we want it to be passed down to the generations."

Bring Your Appetite
as a Guest,
but Leave Your Diet
at Home.

CHEZ NAPOLÉON

365 W. 50TH ST. • NEW YORK, NY 10019

(212) 265-6980 • CHEZNAPOLEON.COM

All the Pieces Fit

At Chez Napoléon, you can order a napoleon. Or "The Coronation of Napoleon." It depends on whether you're in the mood for a dessert or a jigsaw puzzle.

If it's dessert, you would order from the dining menu, which also includes foie gras, coq au vin, and boeuf bourguignon. If it's a jigsaw puzzle, you would order from the jigsaw puzzle menu, which also includes "Le Normandie," "Bal du Moulin," and "Summer in Provence."

Either way, you get something French. And either way, you get something that others may see as outmoded but that can actually be very satisfying. In short, you can indulge in old-time food or an old-time hobby, and you can indulge in either or both in an old-time restaurant.

Chez Napoléon has one of the last of the city's traditional French menus, and what's probably the city's only jigsaw puzzle menu. It has the kind of French food that many people have forsaken for being too rich. They have upgraded to bacon cheeseburgers, fries, and a shake.

But freed of most competition, Chez Napoléon is still cooking, now well past its fiftieth anniversary. It has been refreshed, but you'd hardly know it. You still feel like you're in a French home. Or at least a French home whose decor celebrates the French Revolution.

In that home, you can start with the foie gras or the escargots de Bourgogne, and move on to the boeuf bourguignon, coq au vin, or cuisses de grenouilles. Those are frogs' legs. If that makes you queasy, consider instead the cervelle de veau, foie de veau, or ris de veau, which are the brain, liver, and thymus.

These are classics. But so are the lapin Marguerite ("rabbit served in a light mustard and white wine sauce"), the cassoulet ("white bean stew with duck, lamb, pork cuts, and garlic sausage"), and the bouillabaisse ("the traditional French provincial fish soup event").

In other words, there is plenty for everyone, though less if you happen to be a vegetarian.

It's all what William Welles, one of the owners, calls "French grandma food," which is accurate, since the head chef is his French grandma. She is Marguerite Bruno, better known as Chef Grand-mère, which means "Chef Grandma." She's in her nineties. That's her name on the rabbit. Marguerite owns the restaurant with Elayne Bruno, who's her daughter, and with William, who's Elayne's son. The three generations work together to keep the restaurant quaint yet vital. They may sometimes be generations apart, but it still seems to be working.

Chez Napoléon was launched by a family—not the Brunos, but the Despeaux. They bought a little French restaurant on the site called La Gerbe d'Or. They renamed it for their patriarch, who is said to have evoked the namesake emperor not only in stature but also in temperament. They opened in 1960, which was a good year in that the restaurant was then across the street from Madison Square Garden. Seven years later the Garden moved and the restaurant was across the street from a parking lot. Soon after, the Despeaux sold to another French family.

Soon after that, Marguerite and her husband, Alfred, who had run a restaurant in the Alps, came to America and opened a restaurant in New York. It was L'Esterel, on East 58th Street. Elayne was a waitress there. When it closed, she became a waitress at Chez Napoléon. She and Marguerite bought the restaurant in 1982, in time for recession, soaring rents, and French-food backlash. But there's always something. And Elayne had no patience for the backlash: "I think people have this idea that French food is too rich and too heavy. But French people are not obese like here."

Alfred died in 1992. As for her own husband, Elayne says, "I sent him back to France in 1985." A few years later, William—also known as Guillaume—came on board as the bartender and began sneaking in some new ideas, notably the puzzle menu.

His first jigsaw puzzle was a birthday present from his father twenty years ago. It was a black-and-white portrait of Edith Piaf. He loved it. He wanted more. He wanted everyone to want more. He wanted to print up a puzzle menu. His mother was against it. He did it anyway. It made sense to him, and most of the themes were French. He put a note on the bottom of the food menu that said to ask for the puzzle menu. People asked. Especially after he started framing his finished puzzles and hanging them on the dining room walls.

A recent menu's selections ranged from "Passage Fontaine," which is five hundred pieces and costs $14, to "The Coronation of Napoleon," from the 1806 Jacques-Louis David work, which is six thousand pieces and costs $80.

Like the food, William says, the puzzles appeal to holdouts. In the Depression, he points out, families gathered to put the pieces together. Some customers come in regularly to pick up their next challenge. Some send him pictures of their finished puzzles, though probably not "Passage Fontaine."

Meanwhile, the Bruno family keeps tackling its own challenges, which extend beyond changing tastes and rising rent. They have lost dinner business to the hamburger stands and to the many other new restaurants, and lunch business to takeouts and to office cafeterias.

But they are shielded by their unique attractions, of which there is at least one more: a bar that invites you to sit down and drink by yourself. Its single stool is a rest spot for Chef Grand-mère, but otherwise, Elayne says, it constitutes "the singles bar for people who want to stay single."

DE ROBERTIS PASTICCERIA & CAFFÈ

176 FIRST AVE. • NEW YORK, NY 10009

(212) 674-7137 • DEROBERTISCAFFE.COM

Putting Pastry in Its Place

You can't know that your pastries look good until you've seen them from the front. Annie realizes this. And you've got to admit, her pastries look good.

Annie is Anna De Robertis Mansueto, one of several De Robertises who run De Robertis Pasticceria and Caffè. She learned about pastry from her father. He taught a lot of lessons. But they've helped his bakery to last for several years—into its second century.

De Robertis is your best chance to have pastries from long ago, since it's not only an antique pasticceria but also an antique caffè. The caffè is a gleaming space filled with touches of painstaking workmanship; the pasticceria is a gleaming space filled with touches of Annie's father.

The store opened on April 20, 1904. It was called Caffè Pugliese, for Puglia in Italy. That was the birthplace of the founder, Paolo De Robertis, who was the father of John De Robertis, who was Annie's father and the bakery's backbone. John's pastry rule was common sense, but common sense has never been common. Otherwise, every bakery would be as neat as this. "My father was a meticulous man," Annie says. "He always said that you've got to go to the front of the counter to see how things look."

That's why the trays are always full, and why the pastries that fill them are always carefully arranged. Here you don't see a big, bare tray with three brownies and some petrified crumbs. De Robertis has its pride, no matter what it took to get it.

The pride has not only kept the pastries perfectly piled, but it has also kept the caffè perfectly preserved. It's a classic—a bygone bistro, with lustrous walls that were hand-tiled, from the pressed-tin ceiling to the floor, which was also hand-tiled.

It's a room that takes you back to a time when people cared enough to put some effort into a room for having coffee and pastry. And conveniently, you can sit in that room and have your coffee with a pastry made from a recipe that's probably older than the room.

Among the traditional favorites are sfogliatella, pasticciotti, sassatine Siciliane, and the more universal cannoli. Old-time cookies include quaresemali, savoiarde, anisette, and ossi di morto ("bones of the dead"), which were for All Souls Day but now rattle around all year. There is cuccidate for Christmas, Easter egg bread for Easter, and panettone for both Christmas and Easter. There are sfingi, also known as sfingi di San Giuseppe because they're for St. Joseph's Day, which as luck would have it is a feast day.

To safeguard its past, De Robertis has recognized the present. It has added things that Americans typically want to see. If ossi di morto leave you cold, you can choose from the likes of muffins, turnovers, strudel, cheesecakes, chocolate chip cookies, brownies, and black-and-whites.

On the other hand, if you're hot, De Robertis can cool you off, at least in the summer, with its old-time Italian ices. It has its original flavors of lemon, chocolate, cremolata, and espresso, along with late starters like pineapple, cherry, watermelon, and cantaloupe.

It has ice cream, too, but only a couple of flavors.

Paolo was about pastry. Vito was about ice cream.

Vito was Paolo De Robertis's brother and partner. Together they rented the store on the Lower East Side. Paolo soon returned to Italy, leaving the store to John and Vito. Then Vito left, too. "Vito went to ice cream," Annie says. "He told John, 'Take it, it's yours.'"

John took it, since he did not hear the call of the freezer. But he saw to it that he didn't take it alone. He was assisted by his wife, Antoinette, and later by their children, Anna, Paul, Michael, and John Jr. Annie started working at the store when she was eleven.

John stood up to the Depression, Annie says: "He got me and my brothers through a lot." Along the way, he may also have put them through a lot. But he did it so that they could lead the bakery themselves, which they got the chance to do because he also bought the building.

They would learn that no respectable sugar dispenser is half full. They would learn that no respectable table has crumbs behind the sugar dispenser. They would learn that you "clean up as you go along," even though that's counterintuitive to children. And they would learn that you view the pastries the way the customers are going to view them.

They would also learn things that went beyond aesthetics, to help them become not just good employees but also good employers. That's why, to this day, it's sometimes hard to tell which are which: "My father always said, 'You treat your staff like family.'"

The staff still includes Annie's brothers, as well as the next generation, which is represented by John III. Annie says that he came in understanding what he was in for: "He knows it's a lot of work. He knows you don't have a social life."

Then again, the bakery is a social life. Some regulars come in daily. "Ninety-nine percent of my customers are gems," Annie says.

"I have my mother's habit," she adds. "I kiss everyone. I can't help it. I have a little lady who comes in; she's eighty-seven years old. She reminds me of my grandma."

THE DONUT PUB

203 W. 14TH ST. • NEW YORK, NY 10011

(212) 929-0126 • DONUTPUB.COM

A Glaze of Glory

Dunkin' Donuts does all right for itself—except when it gets around Seventh Avenue and 14th Street. It last got around there in 2007, when it opened a store at 215 West 14th. The store was gone in three years. It couldn't find the doughnut crowd. That's because the crowd was at 203 West 14th, having a cruller and coffee at The Donut Pub.

The battle was almost an even match. Dunkin' Donuts has ten thousand stores; The Donut Pub has one. OK, it wasn't an even match. And yet it was a chain-store massacre. America may run on Dunkin', but New York stops at The Pub.

The Donut Pub is among the last outposts from an era when the city had independent doughnut shops by the dozen. It opened in 1964, which was a while after the first Dunkin', but soon enough to establish itself as the neighborhood place to dunk.

Back then, most people ate their doughnuts in doughnut shops, as opposed to now, when most people take their doughnuts out of doughnut shops. The shops were indeed like pubs—places where you could take a break, sit among others, and have a little something that made you feel better.

The Donut Pub is still like that. It has a nice long counter with stools at which you can commune with the others, or just keep to yourself. Patrons settle in, maybe with a newspaper and usually two pastries, since there are always two that you can't choose between, so you get both.

Among the doughnuts are all the standards, including plain, sugar, cinnamon, honey-dipped, jelly, chocolate, vanilla, chocolate-glazed, and Boston cream. There are also muffins, cupcakes, cookies, very likely the best black-and-white in the city, and doughnut holes, which Dunkin' calls Munchkins and which the Pub calls doughnut holes.

You can start (or finish) with food; the Pub has a lunchbox-sandwich list including cream cheese and jelly, tuna salad, egg salad, ham, and bologna. The sandwiches are just fine. But the sweets are the chain-breakers. Locals have long testified that the doughnuts here are just plain better.

They also testify about the service, which is understandable, since it comes from people like Sam, who's worked the counter for nearly thirty years, and from Gus Markatos, who had a job here when he was in high school and is now an owner, which doesn't keep him from working the counter himself.

"I like interacting with people," Gus says. "When someone's not in, I cover for them. I drink coffee, I eat doughnuts, I do everything." That must please Buzzy Geduld, the owner who founded The Pub and became a Wall Street market-maker yet still holds on to his doughnuts.

For Buzzy, the shop is a symbol of how to do things right, no matter how far up the ladder you think you have climbed. "Business is business, whether it's a brokerage firm or a doughnut shop," he says. "If you put your customers first and watch your p's and q's, people will come back."

Doughnut stores reputedly arrived in New York City in 1931, with a Times Square shop appropriately called Mayflower Doughnuts. Its founder was Adolph Levitt, who invented the first doughnut machine and made Mayflower the country's first doughnut chain.

Dunkin' Donuts began in 1948 in Quincy, Massachusetts, as the Open Kettle, which was wisely renamed in 1950. Its founder was William Rosenberg, who in 1946 had run Industrial Luncheon Services, which sold sandwiches to factory workers.

Buzzy founded The Donut Pub with his brother, Irwin, in '64. Eventually they had eight doughnut shops, but not for long. "We weren't smart enough to even know what a franchise was," Buzzy says. "So we sold them fast. But I kept one in case Wall Street didn't work out."

In the sixties doughnut shops were everywhere, since back then doughnuts were good for you. There were shops all over the neighborhood, Gus says, including across the street. He's not sure how many times Dunkin' Donuts has taken on The Pub, but he knows that it did in the nineties. Also for three years.

In the nineties the vaunted Krispy Kreme Doughnuts arrived in the city. It opened its first store nine blocks away in 1996. The company called itself "the biggest thing to hit New York since Nathan's sold its first hot dog." The Pub would go on to cream Krispy just the way it had slammed Dunkin'.

In 2007, armed with a new slogan, Dunkin' tried again, just a brazen few doors away from The Pub. This time Pub fans got irritated. Some took it as a personal insult. The new store was empty by 2010. For years, all that remained were Dunkin' doorknobs.

The Pub's interior is not original, though people think it is. It's been spruced up. But the place still seems like an old doughnut shop. That, along with its neon sign, adds to its appeal. A chain shop feels like a place to get out of. The Donut Pub feels like a place to come into.

There's no telling whether Dunkin' will try again anyway. As of press time, its store with the doorknobs was still vacant. But a Pub night man advises against it. As he observes, "Why would you try to compete with a place that's been here since '64? Have some respect for the place."

DUPLEX

61 CHRISTOPHER ST. • NEW YORK, NY 10014

(212) 255-5438 • THEDUPLEX.COM

Cabaret Is a Life

ive women take the stage. They are the Panty Hoes. The women sing a song. It's "Black Horse and a Cherry Tree." You probably don't know the song. You surely don't know the Hoes. This is the essence of the Duplex: Everything is a surprise.

The Duplex is a venerable West Village nightspot that's been around for so long that it's turned into a triplex. It has a piano bar and a lounge, which are their own sorts of surprises, but it is legendary for its cabaret, which has had decades of surprises.

New surprises have included a gospel-singing transvestite named Rev. Yolanda, and an elderly psychiatrist and his son in an act called "C'mon, Get Pappy!" Old surprises have included Woody Allen and Joan Rivers, who, at least back then, probably seemed almost as improbable.

The Panty Hoes are part of the Gotham Rock Choir, which bills itself as "New York City's only pop, rock, and soul choir." The five Hoes embody, if inadvertently, the Duplex ethos: Their hair is blond, brunette, red, black, and auburn. Something for everyone.

In various configurations, the choir does a dozen numbers. Its director sings one extolling a vegetarian diet with bacon. The singers don't hit every note. But their cover charge is $12. When they hit every note, they can go to the Café Carlyle and charge a hundred.

The Duplex is a place that generates future entertainment. It's a place that an act can rise from, and there are fewer and fewer of those. "It's kind of a starting place," says the owner, Tony DeCicco, "a place where you can come and get your first audience."

It's an earthy place. It's been in its current home for about twenty years, but you could mistake it for having been there for all of its sixty-year life. In ambience, it recalls old Greenwich Village congeniality. In decor, it recalls old Greenwich Village frugality.

On the ground floor is an ordinary bar that gets extraordinary every night when it turns into the Duplex piano bar. Patrons take the microphone and sing—or belt—their favorites. Sometimes the piano man plays guitar. Sometimes the bartender plays tambourine.

On the next floor is another bar, festive in a different way. It's the lounge, and it hosts what seems like a perpetual wedding reception. Both bars are gay bars. But a few steps down from the lounge is the cabaret, and, just like the Panty Hoes, it has no limits to its appeal.

Despite a formidable succession of owners and managers, the Duplex has managed to end up more or less what it was at the start. And it was compelling enough thirty years ago to inspire an NYU arts student to make it the subject of a 105-page master's thesis. The student, David Diamond, chronicled the nightspot's birth and its bouncy ride through its first three decades (and got his degree). It's the tale of a place that survived not only the vagaries of cabaret, but also bewildering changes in music, culture, the city, and its own name.

The Duplex appears to have made its debut in 1951. It was founded by Jimmy di Martino, at 55 Grove Street. He had a piano bar on the first floor and another bar on the second floor, which, he soon determined, was one bar too many. In 1955 he leased the second floor to three performers: Hal Holbrook, Lovelady Powell, and Brooks Morton. It was around that time that Holbrook launched his one-man show about Mark Twain. He went on to be Mark Twain longer than Mark Twain was Mark Twain.

Powell, a singer affectionately known as "Lovey," opened their show with Morton, her accompanist, and Holbrook closed the show as Twain.

With their performing and management skills, the three made a destination out of the club, which had been redubbed the Upstairs-at-the-Duplex.

But the performers grew increasingly out of tune with the owner, and they left him on his own in 1956. Three years later, di Martino hired a manager named Jan Wallman, who launched what could be called the Duplex's golden age.

Among Wallman's gold was the nightclub debut of Woody Allen, in the early sixties. At the time, Allen was writing for TV stars like Garry Moore. Allen was quoted about those days by Cleveland Amory in the *Newark Evening News* of February 18, 1968:

"I literally had to beg for my first performing job. It was in Greenwich Village, at The Duplex, and they put on anyone who's not a catastrophe. But you get no money at all. At eleven at night, I'd get in a cab in the freezing cold and go down there and perform for nothing for five or six people. Twelve was a big night."

Still, the Duplex was a farm club for tonier spots like the Blue Angel uptown, which is where Allen himself landed next. Jan Wallman left for a couple of years but came back to give early breaks to the likes of Rivers, Dick Cavett, and Rodney Dangerfield.

While she was gone—according to the thesis—the Duplex became the Saint-and-Sinner Room, but the old name was soon back, and so was Wallman. In the seventies, the club was forced to become things like a discotheque. But by 1977 it was again a piano bar and cabaret.

Rick Panson bought the club in 1984 and, amid landlord trouble, moved it in 1989. But like most of its owners, he was wise enough to keep it what it was meant to be, right till he sold it to Tony in 2004.

"It's a terrific icon in longevity, in entertainment, in community spirit," Rick says. "It's a neighborhood club with an international reputation. And it's got a wonderful history, created by the thousands of talented people who make the magic there."

Take Your Sweet Time

*A*s a boy, I cribbed a science report from a Bonomo's Turkish Taffy wrapper. This was dishonest. But so was Bonomo's. It was neither Turkish nor taffy.

In any case, my report was called "How We See," and my source was a feature on the back of the wrapper called "Exciting Science Facts." Bonomo's was the candy you smacked on a table to crack into pieces; thus it not only fed you but relieved your aggressions and did your homework.

These are the sorts of memories that come flooding back to you—whether you want them to or not—in the memory lanes of Economy Candy. It's a confection mine where you can dig up your entire childhood, or start a new one. It's the kid's dream that you couldn't have handled as a kid.

It is famous for being that, but even more famous for being the store where people find candies that they thought had faded away with their youth. It has Bonomo's Turkish Taffy. It has Goldenberg's Peanut Chews. It has Clark Bars, Cherry Mashes, Bit-O-Honeys, Sugar Daddys, Necco Wafers, Red Hots, Nik-L-Nips, and Chuckles.

My science report, or rather Bonomo's, said, "Our eyes tell us about shape, color, size, and distance. They give us knowledge and countless pleasures." I, or rather Bonomo, undoubtedly wrote that with this store in mind, for nowhere are those exciting science facts truer than in here.

You'll see Chiclets and Sixlets; Fizzies and Razzles; Hot Tamales, Idaho Spuds, and Boston Baked Beans. You'll see Zeros and 100 Grands; Rocky

Roads and Skybars; Pixy Stix and Big Hunks; Atomic Fireballs and Milk Duds. You'll see Ring Pops, Blow Pops, Whirly Pops, Tootsie Pops, Pop Rocks, Pez, Chupa Chups, and Abba-Zabas. You'll see candy sticks, candy buttons, candy necklaces, candy Legos, candy cigars, candy cigarettes, chocolate coins, and wax fangs.

Walls are lined with jelly beans, the shiny baubles of candy. The back displays Turkish delights, the luncheon loaves of candy. There are bushels of nuts and dried fruits, and cases of hand-dipped chocolates—along with old comic books and candy vending machines, to augment your trip to the past.

"How We See" notwithstanding, visitors don't believe their eyes. The store owner, Jerry Cohen, says that some think the candy's antique. "They ask, 'Is this still made?' 'Where did you find it?' and 'Is it edible?' When they start asking me how many calories, I tell them, 'This is the wrong store for you.'"

The candy is all still made, but some makers don't make a lot. Many formerly big brands have turned into little brands. Jerry helps keep them alive, which is why you find brands you thought were dead, like Hopjes, Charms, Chunky, Black Jack, and Sen-Sen.

Economy has a few bigger names, but even those seem more magical here. Since there's little else but candy, the candy seems more important. And it really is economical, because Jerry buys so much. "No one can match our prices," he says. It's one reason no one can match their history.

Economy was born in 1937 (around the time the Bonomo family bought M. Schwarz & Sons' Turkish Chewing Taffy). It was owned by Hyman Russo, who was the father of Sam Russo, who was the brother-in-law of Moishe Cohen, who was Jerry's father.

The original store (whose name is apparently lost to time) was at the corner of Rivington and Essex Streets. It was a shoe store that sold candy until the shoes were outsold by the candy, even though there were lots of other stores on other corners selling candy.

After the war, Moishe and his wife, Joan, ran the store with Sam. Moishe and Joan were joined by their kids, Jerry, Bernice, and Suzanne. Eventually, Bernice and Suzanne left, and later Sam did, too. Now the store is run by Jerry and his wife, Ilene.

In the early days, Jerry says, besides the candy inside the store, there were carts of candy, dried fruits, and nuts outside the store. "I always felt bad for my father standing outside in the wintertime," he says. He vowed not to go into the business himself. He went into it anyway.

In 1985, he says, the rent on the store was about to triple, so he packed up all the candy and moved it to the current address. And he did his best to make up for his father's winters on the sidewalk by packing him up and sending him to Florida.

Now Jerry is looking forward to retirement himself, and he has lined up an unexpected replacement: his son, Mitchell. "Kids don't want to take over parents' businesses," he says. "Kids are lawyers, kids are doctors. My son is unusual in that he wants to come back."

The future thus ensured, Jerry can enjoy his work. He has no need to expand the store or to open other ones. He loves the one store, and he loves one time of year there in particular: "Halloween. It's just a wonderful holiday. It's the one holiday when everybody has to have candy."

EISENBERG'S SANDWICH SHOP

174 FIFTH AVE. • NEW YORK, NY 10010

(212) 675-5096 • EISENBERGSNYC.COM

Keep the Change

The secret to making great egg salad is to mix eggs with mayonnaise. The secret to making great tuna salad is to mix tuna with mayonnaise. The secret to making a great egg salad or tuna salad sandwich is to put egg salad or tuna salad between two slices of bread.

You may have known these secrets. And yet you are not famous for your salad sandwiches, while Eisenberg's Sandwich Shop is. This is because you don't serve your sandwiches in the Flatiron District, at a lunch counter from the twenties with a rail for people's feet.

Though it's been through several owners, Eisenberg's has managed to remain the sandwich place that's a perfect complement to its town. It keeps its food simple in a city where everything else is complicated. It sells a tuna sandwich. Not a tuna wrap. Not a tuna panini.

It's like a neighborhood bar except with lime rickeys and egg creams on tap—a New York luncheonette where you feel like you're lunching with New York. You know it's special and you know that the other people there know it's special. And you also know this doesn't mean you have to talk to them.

In short, it's a classic sandwich shop that makes just the classic sandwiches—ham, cheese, ham and cheese, bologna, salami, liverwurst, turkey, chicken, roast beef, sardines, peanut butter and jelly. And shrimp salad. But only on Friday.

It also has Jewish deli sandwiches—corned beef, pastrami, brisket, tongue. Outside of those, however, its most exotic offering is the Cuban. It wasn't until around 2006 that, by popular demand, it added an upstart sandwich that seemed to be catching on elsewhere. It was called a hamburger.

As for the place, it's essentially an endless black marble counter with swiveling stools, though not a lot of space for swiveling. Across from the counter are little tables. If you plan to walk between the stools and the tables when you're done eating, don't eat a lot. Occupying that counter and those tables through the years have been working New Yorkers seeking familiar food in familiar surroundings. Among them was Josh Konecky, who in 2005 did what he had to do to keep the food and the surroundings familiar.

He was in printing, but he had always wanted to be in food. Printing wasn't going so well—and neither, it seemed, was Eisenberg's. The previous owner didn't fit, he says: "He couldn't schmooze. This is a business where you have to schmooze. So I thought, 'Why don't you just buy Eisenberg's?'"

The Eisenbergs, who opened the place around 1929, had been gone for decades. But they left a place that they had mostly left alone. The next owners embraced that tradition, whether through reverence or inertia. Eisenberg's was lucky. Josh meant to keep it that way.

"There was a lot I had to do to clean it up," he says. "The regulars said, 'You're gonna change it!' I said, 'I'm just gonna clean it up.'" He cleaned it up. The regulars stayed. He raised the prices. They still stayed. He added the burger. They kept staying. After all, it's the Eisen-Burger.

"I was worried what was going to happen when the old-timers die off," Josh admits. "But kids love this place. It's about what your sensibilities are, what kind of person you are." His motto has appeared on the chalkboard out on the sidewalk: "Eisenberg's: You either get it or you don't."

Paul Ginsburg has gotten it for about half a century. He's been eating at Eisenberg's since he was seven. He is a clothier and the son of the late Moe Ginsburg, who ran the eponymous men's store that became an Eisenberg's neighbor in the seventies.

Vintage Spot: Chelsea

EL QUIJOTE: EST. 1930

The name suggests a theme. The interior hollers it. This is the truly quixotic place for Spanish cuisine. Whether in the Don Quijote Room, the Dulcinea Room, or the Cervantes Room, you're among Quixote statuary and murals of windmills, including one whose sails really spin.

226 W. 23rd St.; (212) 929-1855; elquijoterestaurant.com

"Eisenberg's, in the early days, was considered a haven for the Jewish immigrants, the Russian immigrants, who owned and worked and operated the tailored men's business," Paul says. "They conducted business in the back. What made it great for them was that it was wholesome, affordably priced, and quick."

"The countermen were characters in their own right," he adds. "They were right out of the *Grumpy Old Men* movie. Tourists either loved it or wanted to punch the countermen out. I just remember the hustle and the bustle, all the good-natured noise."

He says that Josh "understands the responsibility of Eisenberg's"—which he apparently does, since he still hasn't added wraps or paninis. In fact, Josh says, he added burgers only to be responsible: Too many potential customers were walking out because he had none.

Josh has lined the wall with pictures of himself with stars—but that's tradition. And he has added to the store's two slogans—but that's pride. He's kept "Continuous Fine Quality." He's kept "Fine Quality Food." He just added: "Raising New York's Cholesterol Since 1929."

It Can Make Your Year

Even the powerful need a place where everybody knows their names, which is why the midday meal at The Four Seasons should be called the pamper lunch. But of course, it's the power lunch, though people lunch there less to be powerful than to be welcomed, acknowledged, and indulged.

Oliver Stone said that The Four Seasons reminded him of his high-school cafeteria, since it, too, tends to get the same kids every day. But it's also different. The furniture's better. The kids' clothes are nicer. And a piece of apple pie costs a whole week's allowance.

The clientele has changed since the restaurant opened in 1959. Power mostly resides in different places now. The diners once were largely publishers, writers, and ad men. Now they're largely real-estate magnates, bank magnates, and hedge-fund magnates.

But their room is the same, and their goals are the same: to see, to be seen, and to be served. Deals are done, but deal-making is just part of the deal. The term "power lunch" doesn't get to the heart of the place, according to at least one man who does.

"It's hard to grasp what this room means to the occupants," says Alex von Bidder, one of The Four Seasons' owners. "This room is important to those people. That's why they come. Their placement is important to them. They all know each other. They go to the same parties. They do business with each other."

The restaurant is unique not just in significance but in atmosphere. It's vast yet cozy; open yet private; stately yet restrained. It's been called the greatest dining room in the city, and it might be. In fact, it might be the two greatest dining rooms in the city.

The power room is the Grill Room, or Bar Room. It's the one with the French-walnut panels, the shimmering chain-curtains, and the clusters of dangling bronze rods. It's where the seats at the five booths at the center are the virtual thrones. At lunch you don't get those seats. You are given those seats.

But past a hallway hung with a giant Picasso stage curtain is the Pool Room—less powerful, perhaps, but arguably more resplendent. There, besides a window view, you have a water view, supplied by a bubbling white marble pool surrounded by lofty potted trees. The Pool Room is preferred by the powerful who want to be left alone. It's preferred by most people for dinner, as well as for weddings and bar mitzvahs. It's the better room for fashion shows, and it's the better room for lunch if you don't feel up to trying to be important.

Regardless of your room, you will be cared for in a manner befitting someone who may be spending a couple of hundred for a meal. But The Four Seasons was not created to be a dining club for the rich. It was created simply to be the greatest restaurant in the world.

The creators were Jerry Brody and Joe Baum, who'd launched a restaurant revolution through the storied company Restaurant Associates. Their dress rehearsal was a lavish proto-theme restaurant in Rockefeller Center lavishly called The Forum of the Twelve Caesars.

From The Forum they may have determined that New York was less in need of twelve Caesars than of something quintessentially New York. That's what they went for when they got the job of installing a showplace in Ludwig Mies van der Rohe's modernist Seagram Building.

They hired the architect Philip Johnson, who'd had a hand in the building. For every task, in fact, they hired the best, since that's what Seagram wanted. Along the way, Baum was supposedly charmed by a haiku about the four seasons. They briefly considered names like The Coliseum of the Four Seasons.

But they chose understatement, which is why they chose the panels for the walls and the rod sculptures by Richard Lippold to crown the terrace and the bar. Lippold also suggested window curtains of necklace-like chains. When they were hung, thanks to physics, they rippled like waterfalls.

The same attention was given to accoutrements from the chairs to the matchbooks, many of which would appropriately change their looks with the seasons. The restaurant reportedly cost $4.5 million, which reportedly was a record. And it reportedly kept costing more.

It was an artistic and culinary hit, of course, but not a financial one. Though its reputation grew steadily, its profits did not. A succession of directors made a succession of changes, but by the seventies The Four Seasons, like the city it had sought to symbolize, was under a cloud.

The men who got it out were the new owners, Tom Margittai and Paul Kovi, who proceeded to court editors, writers, and publishers. They hired Alex, who had a flair for nurturing the banquet business, and Julian Niccolini, who had a flair for nurturing power.

In 1979 *Esquire* ran a story that called The Four Seasons the home of the "power lunch." According to *The Four Seasons,* by John Mariani with Alex, "Suddenly, to all the world The Four Seasons Bar Room was where everybody with aspirations to power, money, and glamour wanted to be between noon and three."

The Four Seasons—after two decades—was indeed one of the most famous restaurants in the world, and it's managed to stay that way since. In 1995 Alex and Julian became the new owners, and they've been careful to keep it the kind of place where power likes to lunch.

"It's a simple business," Alex says. "You listen to your customers. As they say, the taste of the roast depends on the greeting of the host."

GALLAGHER'S STEAK HOUSE

228 W. 52ND ST. • NEW YORK, NY 10019

(212) 245-5336 • GALLAGHERSNYSTEAKHOUSE.COM

Dinner of Champions

*A*t lots of restaurants, the waiters can't tell you what happened three days ago. At Gallagher's, the waiters can tell you what happened three decades ago.

Mario Gonzalez, for instance, can tell you what happened when Muhammad Ali was there—and a waiter named Ali was also there. A phone call came. The maître d' hurried to the champ's table with the telephone and announced, "This is your brother from Egypt."

Mario has stories like that because he's been a waiter here for four decades, which is possible because Gallagher's has been here for nine decades. "I take care of queens, kings," Mario says. "One time I served the Prince of Monaco. I take care of so many big names."

Among other big names waiters drop are Frank Sinatra, Elizabeth Taylor, Bing Crosby, James Cagney, Paul Newman, Jacqueline Onassis, and John F. Kennedy Jr. Gallagher's Steak House has long been a place where big names can come to relax and forget, for a while, that their names are big.

"One night I spent a few hours with Richard Burton," Mario says. "After a while, he started singing." A waiter named George has an indelible memory of George C. Scott: "If there was a lot of noise, he would say 'Shaddup!' and everybody was quiet."

Gallagher's is in the theater district, so it's been a natural for show people, but it was also around the corner from the old Madison Square Garden.

So it also welcomed the likes of Mickey Mantle, Joe DiMaggio, Joe Louis, Jack Dempsey, Wilt Chamberlain, and Arnold Palmer.

It's one of those places that take you back before you get in; you get in through one of the last of the city's wooden revolving doors. You're then surprised by the see-through meat locker, and finally by a cavernous space that might be described as Old New York meets the Ponderosa.

Under your feet are plank floors; over your head are log lights. In between are knotty-pine walls and tables with red gingham tablecloths. On the walls are hundreds of framed pictures, portraits, and posters of mostly forgotten actors, politicians, businessmen, and racehorses. Filling one of the walls is the Canvas of Stars, a mural by the artist Peb. It imagines a party attended by seventy-three famous Gallagher's regulars. Front and center among the revelers are Jerry and Marlene Brody, which is appropriate, since they're the couple who made the party possible.

Gallagher's got its name from Helen Gallagher, a former Ziegfeld girl who opened it as a speakeasy in 1927. She got her name from Edward Gallagher, of vaudeville's Gallagher and Shean, who were famous for their signature song, "Mister Gallagher and Mister Shean."

But Mr. Gallagher and Mrs. Gallagher ended their marriage, and Helen opened her place with a bookie named Jack Solomon. After Prohibition, Helen and Jack turned Gallagher's into a steakhouse. Helen died in 1943, but her first husband's name lived on. Jack died in 1963, but not before gaining the distinction of having married two former Ziegfeld girls in a row. The second was Irene Hayes, who went on to become a Park Avenue florist and, upon Jack's death, the owner of a steakhouse.

That made one business too many, so she put the steakhouse on the block. She sold it to Jerry Brody, the restaurant impresario. Brody had already led the team that created The Four Seasons, and would go on to rescue the Grand Central Oyster Bar & Restaurant.

In the Helen-and-Jack days, the restaurant had profited from, besides the old Garden, a theater district that had dozens of shows running at once.

It also drew Jack's friends, who tended to be other gamblers, and Helen's friends, who tended to be Ziegfeld girls, who in turn drew their admirers.

But under Jack, the magic had faded. In Brody's biography, *A Time Well Spent,* Lawrence Freundlich describes Brody's new purchase: "The staff of waiters was down to six from sixteen. After 9:00 PM, only two waiters worked and the staff would lay green mats on the dining tables and play cards."

"On the first night he owned it, we had dinner there," Marlene Brody recalls. "There were four other men eating there, and they were all bookies." Part of the dining area was closed off with a curtain, she adds: "He took it down and said the room was going to be full again."

He was right. It was full again, and by 1966 Princess Grace was hiring Gallagher's to cater her summer barbecue. When everything was under control, Brody moved on to the Oyster Bar and, with Marlene, became an Angus breeder and then a Thoroughbred breeder.

Brody died in 2001, and Marlene took over. In early 2013 she sold Gallagher's to the restaurateur Dean Poll. To run a restaurant, she says, "you need money and you need youth. What I really want to do is to breed a champion racehorse."

Fortunately, what Dean really wants to do is to run Gallagher's—and fortunately, he wants it run it more or less as Gallagher's. "It will unquestionably be recognized as a restaurant that's eighty-five years old," he says. "We will certainly maintain its heritage."

"It needs some work," he also says. "But I'm not going to make it into a brand-new, shiny lawyer restaurant. You will know you're in Gallagher's, and you will know you're in a place that has connections to theater, sports, and politics."

"That reassures me," Marlene says, "not because I don't want it to change, but because when people redo things completely and just keep the name, the place loses its soul."

She adds: "The meat locker, he has to leave. It's the only restaurant in the world that has that. People come to take pictures of that."

GEM SPA

131 SECOND AVE. • NEW YORK, NY 10003

(212) 995-1866

For the Serious Drinker

Gem Spa has no gem and isn't a spa, and an egg cream has no egg and isn't a cream. It's no wonder they've stayed together so long. Everyone loves two good mysteries.

Gem Spa is a newsstand on the corner of Second Avenue and St. Mark's Place. It looks like a newsstand, or at least a newsstand with a bazaar. But it has distinguished itself with a specialty, rendered on plastic above its awning and promised on the awning itself: NEW YORK'S BEST EGG CREAM.

An egg cream is a drink made by mixing chocolate syrup, milk, and seltzer. It looks like chocolate milk, or at least chocolate milk with a white hat. It is a part of New York history, even though no one is sure of its history. Correctly made, it's delicious. But it's often incorrectly made.

In the old days it was often correctly made, because it was made everywhere, at least in this neighborhood. You could get it not only in restaurants but also routinely at newsstands. But the culture that made it dispersed. The drink survived, but it eventually became just another coffee-shop beverage.

But not at Gem Spa.

Walk in. That is, work your way past the scarves, sunglasses, fanny packs, flip-flops, bandannas, and baseball caps, and walk in. Browse the full line of periodicals. Pick up things you're short on, like shoelaces, rubber bands, safety pins, birthday candles, dominoes, and chalk. Then go to the counter. Look down and see a tiny, almost hidden soda fountain. Make your request, and a counter person will make you a taste of the past. And it's likely to be correctly made, because the Gem Spa management recognizes that egg creams are a significant part of its bread and butter.

"This is known to the whole country," says Ray, the current owner, who doesn't even like to say "Ray" because he wants people to think "Gem." "People come to drink our egg cream from Texas, California, Europe, everywhere. And once they have the egg cream, they have to come back and have it again."

In truth, of course, such a thing as New York's best egg cream is elusive. An egg cream is made by hand and, even at Gem Spa, by various chefs. You can therefore get an egg cream at Gem Spa that isn't quite New York's best, and you could get one at a coffee shop that is, though probably by accident.

That said, Gem Spa's a good bet, because it is built on its egg cream—though, as with the drink, a lot of its history is built on guesses.

New York magazine ran a story about what was then called Gems Spa, titled "Anatomy of a Candy Store," on June 2, 1969. It quotes the owner at the time, Ruby Silverstein, as saying that he bought the lease in 1957, after the store had been run for thirty years by a family named Goldfeather.

Ruby and his partner, Harold Shepard, it says, named their store after Ruby's wife, a former partner's wife, and Harold's wife. The ladies were Gladys, Etta, and Miriam. That gave the men "Gem," to which they added their shared initial, S, and a word that Ruby liked, "spa." Thus, Gems Spa.

The *New York* piece says: "Gems Spa is probably the busiest and the most profitable old-style candy store in the city." But the piece barely mentions egg creams. Back then, the drink was more available and less nostalgic. Still, Ruby apparently did well enough to vacation in the Bahamas.

Ray took over in the eighties, by which time it was Gem Spa. The egg cream technique has reportedly been passed down from owner to owner. But one thing is certain: The newsstand has been a haunt to poets and punks, Beats and bums, hippies and hipsters, and even groups that don't alliterate.

As for the egg cream, one thing is certain about it, too: Outside of its existence, little about it is certain. Like many things whose facts are lost, it has had millions of words written about it, all of which lead to the same conclusion: Your guess is as good as mine. Briefly, the egg cream was almost certainly a contribution of the Jewish immigrant culture of the Lower East Side. A common claim to its invention is that of a family named Auster, who contended that the drink was dreamed up by Louis Auster in a candy store near Gem Spa.

Whoever invented it almost certainly did so around the turn of the last century. In any case, it was at its peak in the middle decades of the century. As Jews moved up and out, the city egg cream was increasingly left in the hands of those less practiced in blending syrup, milk, and fizz.

Regarding the name, there are plenty of theories about that, too, each one as wobbly as the one before. But there's actual evidence to suggest that the drink once did contain egg and cream, which is easier to swallow than the theory that the name came from the French *chocolat et crème.*

In any case, today there are egg-cream rules, not that they necessarily reflect any original egg-cream rules. An egg cream, for instance, should be made with Fox's U-bet Chocolate Flavor Syrup, which means that it should also be chocolate. An egg cream should be made with whole milk and with pressurized seltzer. An egg cream should be in a glass, though one rule says straight and one says curved.

There are rules about the amount, order, and blending of the ingredients. But if everyone followed all the rules, there would hardly be any egg creams. There would be none at Gem Spa, because they make theirs in paper cups. They also make four flavors. And they won't tell what syrup they use.

Ray won't even let you take a picture of his fountain, and he'd prefer that you not look while your egg cream is being made. But he's just protecting the mysteries. You don't know what you're getting, where it came from, or how it's made. That's vintage New York.

Cupcakes Have Their Limits

It was near closing time on a Friday but Herb Glaser was going to bake chocolate chip cookies because he knew that he couldn't send Joseph home cookieless twice.

Joseph was a four-year-old who came to Glaser's Bake Shop on Fridays and ordered a chocolate chip cookie, a choice that confirmed his good taste. He came in that day, but the place had run out. There was no telling what he'd have done if he didn't get his cookie the next day, and Herb Glaser didn't want to find out.

"I'm amazed at how regular people are," Herb said on his way to the dough. "The girls here are like bartenders. They know what people want when they walk in the door." So he plans ahead. But sometimes he's caught short. And when he is, his response often transcends apology.

This is one reason that Glaser's has lived to serve the Josephs of its neighborhood for well over a century. Another is that it has preserved its looks. Another is that it has preserved its recipes. And the main reason is that those recipes make you a regular before you're four.

Though people do have their routines, they can be prompted to change them depending on the aroma in the store, Herb says. "Customers come in, sniff around, and say, 'What are you baking right now?' I say, 'Well, you can't have it, 'cause it's not finished.'"

Among the ways that Glaser's has resisted New York City bakery fashion is to not turn into a cupcake shop. It offers choices beyond cupcake-icing color. Its cases display—along with cupcakes—brownies, éclairs, Danishes, rugalach, black-and-whites, and, most days, chocolate chip cookies. They also display cakes, pies, buns, loaves, rings, horns, crescents, breads, rolls, turnovers, and puffs—along with traditional favorites like Linzer tarts, lace cookies, Bavarian heart cookies, Bavarian almond cookies, and Herb's favorite, Viennese butter pecan cookies.

The nostalgic goods are nicely complemented by the nostalgic decor, which is unique in its theme of 1918 meets 1965. The theme reflects the wisdom of a family that recognized the need for change yet sensed the value of leaving things alone.

John Glaser, born in Bavaria, opened his first Manhattan bakery in the 1890s, in the vicinity of Bloomingdale's, at 60th Street. In 1902 he moved the store to the current location, in the Yorkville neighborhood enclave that was known as Germantown. In 1918 he decided to remodel, which likely as not meant that he decided to finally fix the place up. He installed stately oak cabinets and cases, and a ceramic floor in which little blue tiles spelled out the words "John Glaser Inc."

Herb's father, Herbert, took over the bakery when John died in the thirties, and pretty much left it alone till the sixties. In 1965 he took down the neon sign and replaced it with a plastic one. But the plastic one's as old now as the neon one was then, and Herb, who still favors rotary telephones, plans to leave it alone. Herbert also replaced the display cases (though not the stately oak ones), and over time he laid a few layers of linoleum over the floor tiles. But in the eighties, Herb pulled up all of the linoleum layers and once again exposed the founder's name. Some mistakes can be corrected.

Herb had planned to go to dental school but the waiting list was too long, so he joined the bakery. The jokes about that are too easy. He and his brother, John, took over in the seventies. They are now the owners and bakers, and also the beneficiaries of their forebears' light touch.

"When I was a kid, I thought it would be neat to renovate the place, to make it all new," Herb acknowledges as he surveys his antique store. "Now

I'm very happy that my father didn't do it." His happiness is apparently shared by most of his customers.

The old cabinets are used to honor the shop. They hold photos, clippings, ledgers, and—most bittersweet—a price list from 1966. It offers rolls for 9 cents (now $1), chocolate éclairs for 18 cents (now $2.75), and an eight-inch buttercream birthday cake for $3 (now $30).

Of course, inflation hit everybody. What didn't hit everybody was the decline late last century in purchases at bakeries. Some people abandoned cake and pie; others at least cut back. "Now people are looking for smaller portions," Herb says. "They used to want large cakes; now they want small ones."

Other neighborhood bakeries closed, but supermarket bakeries opened, as did catering companies that ate up the birthday-party business. Herb and John can thank their grandfather for buying their building for an amount closer to today's price of a birthday cake than to today's price of their building. Because of that, they can afford not only to stay in business, but also to bake chocolate chip cookies just for Joseph. They don't have to do all the stuff that most businesses have to do. They can just bake things and sell them to the neighborhood.

They don't take credit cards. They don't deliver. They don't sell franchises. They don't have air-conditioning. They close for all of July and for part of August. John's son, Tom, has joined the business, and he keeps an eye on the competition. But they don't have to worry about competition.

There's still pressure to cut corners, Herb says. "But I've got to be comfortable doing what I'm doing. I sleep well at night. I'm a proud baker. I'm proud of what I do."

The one thing he has cut is his weight. At one point, he hit three hundred.

"I nibble while I work," he says. "There's enough variety that you can always find something."

GRAND CENTRAL
OYSTER BAR & RESTAURANT

LOWER LEVEL, GRAND CENTRAL TERMINAL
89 E. 42ND ST. • NEW YORK, NY 10017
(212) 490-6650 • OYSTERBARNY.COM

Pearl of the Terminal

If you're a connoisseur of oysters or ceilings, you're in luck at the Oyster Bar. If you're a connoisseur of oysters *and* ceilings, you're in more luck at the Oyster Bar. Every day it gives you a choice of about thirty oysters, and every day it gives you a chance to look at a great ceiling.

The Oyster Bar is the cavernous anchor restaurant of the cavernous Grand Central Terminal. It has been so since the two opened in 1913. It is famous for its seafood, but it is also famous for one of the most uplifting canopies of any dining hall in New York City.

The place is indeed a hall; it seats about four hundred people, and it serves about two thousand people a day. And most sit under the five vaults of herringbone terra-cotta tiles that may remind them of Ellis Island's Great Hall, since it has that ceiling, too. The ceiling is by the Guastavino family, who also lent their touch to city landmarks including Carnegie Hall and the Cathedral Church of St. John the Divine. It seems to tell you that you matter, even if you only get soup. It beckons you to come in, even if you don't like fish.

If you do come in and you don't like fish, you still have five menu choices. But you're better off if you do like fish; then you have 140 choices. With due respect to the ceiling, it's the variety that makes the bar, according to at least one of its owners.

Vintage Spots: Midtown East

JIMBO'S HAMBURGER PLACE: EST. 1955

The interior is like new, but you never really notice, since you're engulfed by perpetual hamburger haze. The menu lists twenty-three burgers, made of "The Best Chopmeat Money Can Buy." And yet Jimbo's is also "The Famous Place for Eggs & Omelets."

991 First Ave.; (212) 355-6120; jimboshamburgerplace.com

KING COLE BAR AT THE ST. REGIS HOTEL: EST. 1948

It's often just a noisy bar—but at least it's a noisy bar with a 1906 Maxfield Parrish painting of Old King Cole. And its signature is the Bloody Mary, which may have been invented by a St. Regis bartender, and which was briefly and more politely known as the Red Snapper.

2 E. 55th St.; (212) 753-4500; kingcolebar.com

THE PALM COURT AT THE PLAZA: EST. 1907

You feel rich just sitting below the radiant stained-glass dome among the marble columns, arches, mirrors, statuary, and yes, palms. But it helps to be rich. A two-egg breakfast is $25 (though oatmeal is only $16), and the famous afternoon tea is $50. And up.

768 Fifth Ave.; (212) 546-5300; theplazany.com

THE PALM RESTAURANT: EST. 1926

"Palm" is what the licensing clerk heard when the Italian founders said "Parma," so Palm is the name their restaurant got. It's now a steak house chain, but this is the original, and its walls still display the colorful funnies that working cartoonists drew to pay for their meals.

837 Second Ave.; (212) 687-2953; thepalm.com

"We have thirty different kinds of fish along with thirty different kinds of oysters every day," says Sandy Ingber, the executive chef. "Everything is fresh, fresh, fresh. And we have truth in advertising. When we say it's wild salmon, it's wild salmon. That's how we keep our reputation."

A new menu is printed daily, and a lot changes besides the date. "Raw Bar" may feature Lady Chatterley one day and Peconic Pearl the next. You can always get specialties like oyster stew and oyster panroast, but the seafood choices can leave you at sea—just like the seating choices.

To your left, as you enter, is a dining room full of tables with the traditional red-and-white tablecloths. But to your right are four horseshoe counters, and across from those is the long oyster bar itself, and they all seem like a bit more fun than a dining room. Between the tables and the counters is what looks like an airport lounge, which is also available for your dining pleasure, as is the Saloon, which is in the room beyond the horseshoe counters and is more intimate than the dining room, though it doesn't have the ceiling.

It could take the better part of a lunch hour to pick a chair and a fish. But that's nothing compared with what it has taken the Oyster Bar to survive. Before the hot dog, the pretzel, or the slice, the city's emblematic food was the oyster. Lots of oysters lived here when the city offered cleaner places to live. In the nineteenth century, they were sold in oyster palaces, oyster cellars, oyster saloons, and oyster stands. When the Oyster Bar arrived, it was already late.

But it wasn't too late to be credible, even if the bivalves were no longer locals. And it had the bonus of being surrounded by a majestic new depot. People poured into Grand Central, and they all had to eat. And their decisions were easier then. The Oyster Bar sold mostly oysters.

It was run first by Viktor Yesensky and then by Nick Rossetos. But as train travel lost popularity, so did the bar. By the seventies it needed a savior. Fortunately, one was available. Having rescued Gallagher's Steak House, Jerry Brody was ready for seafood.

Brody, who had also led the creation of showplaces like The Four Seasons, took on the reinvention of a restaurant that had already closed. Among what was left were marble arches plastered with aquamarine contact paper, and a Guastavino tile ceiling obliterated by black grime. With his wife, Marlene, Brody toured the East Coast to find the best fish, and the vineyards of California to find the best wine. In 1974 he opened the Grand Central Oyster Bar & Restaurant as a seafood palace for all people, whether they rode on trains or not.

Needless to say, he also fixed the place up, which proved to be good experience for when he would have to do it again. In 1997 the Oyster Bar had a fire that virtually melted its interior. Practically everything was destroyed. Brody once more rebuilt.

He found a factory that could reproduce the Guastavino tiles. He replaced whatever he could and tried to improve on what he couldn't. Among the new fixtures are the ship's-wheel chandeliers and the barroom plaques with portraits of ships like the Maine sardine carrier *Grayling*.

Brody kept an eye on things until he died, in 2001. The Oyster Bar became the property of its employees, headed by a team including Sandy. Before Brody died, however, the restaurant surprised him by adding another new fixture: a portrait of him over the bar.

Of course, in making the bar a better place, Brody made it a pricier place. Most entrees now hover around $30; appetizers can exceed $15. "You can go there and spend a lot of money," Marlene Brody acknowledges. "Or you can sit at the counter and have a cup of chowder."

That'll run you only about $6, which is a small price to pay to sit under a ceiling that was good enough to be rescued twice.

"My husband set out to make it a destination restaurant, not just a station restaurant," Marlene says. "And he succeeded. It's known the world over now."

HEIDELBERG RESTAURANT

1648 SECOND AVE. • NEW YORK, NY 10028
(212) 628-2332 • HEIDELBERGRESTAURANT.COM

A Country in the City

Once upon a time, there was a place called Germantown. All that's left of it now is a plate of schnitzel. The end.

Well, there's wiener schnitzel, paprika schnitzel, jaeger schnitzel, and à la Holstein schnitzel. And bauernwurst, bratwurst, knackwurst, and weisswurst. And sauerbraten, schweinebraten, Kasseler Rippschen, and Schweine Haxe. But they're all in one place. The last place. The Heidelberg.

It's the sole surviving restaurant of that Yorkville neighborhood enclave, which was a hub of German life in the middle of the last century. The only other German outpost is Schaller & Weber, the nearby butcher, which opened in 1937 but still won't let you eat in.

The Heidelberg sits you down and surrounds you with the old country, from its painting of the Königssee to its needlepoint of the Alps. It offers you spaetzle. It offers you strudel. It offers you beer in a two-liter boot. It sends you waitresses in dirndls, and waiters in lederhosen. It's a perpetual German party complete with a summer biergarten, a laughing ghost that remains defiantly full of life. It has often been close to extinction, but it just keeps coming back. A last place is last for a reason, and the reason is usually family.

"We want to maintain something that was started by our parents and our grandparents," says Dieter Weber, the new chef and the nephew of the owner. "I'm a classically trained chef. I could work anywhere, at double the money. But I choose to stay here because it's where my family is. It's my home."

It's lots of people's home, says Kathy Jolowicz, the Yorkville historian. "If we lost the Heidelberg, I don't know what I'd do. It's a meeting ground for the old Germans. It's the only place in Yorkville that we can come together and talk the language."

They are likely to talk with their mouths full, since Dieter is out to make his food irresistible, whether you're an old German or not. His specialties include the sauerbraten, the schweinebraten (roast loin of pork), and the Schweine Haxe (roasted pork shank), all based on his grandparents' recipes. Some come for those kinds of specialties, some come for the other kinds—the ones with names like Spaten Lager and Bitburger Pils. The Heidelberg has a bar along with the biergarten. Every day is Oktoberfest—just as it was all over the neighborhood.

A century ago the area was filled with German-speaking immigrants, including workers from "Little Germany" on the Lower East Side, Kathy says. "Every establishment was German-speaking. All the shop owners were your neighbors. You lived together, you worked together. Your family were shop owners."

By the thirties, 86th Street was a wonderland of German restaurants, dinner theaters, movie palaces, dance halls, and singing clubs. Their names were on the order of the Jaegerhaus, the Rheinland, the Platzl, and Kleine Konditorei. All have since vanished.

"When I was little I remember seeing people walking down the street in their costumes," Kathy says. "Christmas was the most beautiful. It was more German than Germany. We had lights going over the road, and gingerbread houses. Every place was decorated. It was another world."

A German haunt is believed to have opened in the Heidelberg's space around 1902. It eventually took on the name of Café Vaterland. By the late thirties that name, which means "fatherland," had diminishing allure, and it was changed to the less-patriotic Heidelberg.

Horst and Luise Edler bought the Heidelberg in 1964 (and a few years later wisely bought the building). Through the years, various family members have worked at the restaurant, but the Edlers' eventual successor was their daughter Eva Matischak.

In 1988 Luise was ready to sell. Eva worked hard to make the place more salable. She planned to do that for a year. She's been doing it for fifteen years. She became the official owner in 2001. In 2012, worn down by challenges led by the construction of a new subway line, Eva herself was ready to sell. She planned to do it right away. Instead, she renovated. "I'm very traditional and very loyal," she says. "It was very hard for me to just disappear like that."

She brought back Dieter, who'd peeled potatoes at the place when he was eight, and who'd gone on to run the family's Café Heidelberg in Florida. She also brought in her son, Andreas, who's a helicopter pilot but apparently had time for the family business while on the ground.

The family's determination seems shared by the staff—even the ones who have to dress up. Hannah Sprung, for instance, claims that she's perfectly comfortable in her dirndl. "People like it," she says. "They find it sexy for some reason. I wouldn't mind wearing it in the street, but I don't."

"What I really think is important is to give people something that is real," Eva says. "You can come in here and be yourself. It's not fashionable. It still has a heart and soul. It's not just a place where you come in to eat. It's like coming home. It's like coming home to mother."

ZAGAT RATED
ZAGAT RATED
ZAGAT RATED
RATED
OPEN
ZAGAT RATED
ZAGAT RATED

NO CDs NO TAPES
VINYL RULES

DISCOVER
MasterCard
VISA

ZAGAT RATED

LARGEST
SELECTION
OF
XMAS
RECORDS
IN NEW YORK

WEDNESDAY MORNING, 3AM
SIMON & GARFUNKEL

BOBBY D

CIRCLE CLUB

NO CD'S
NO TAPES

Largest Sele
OF
RARE
SOUND TRA
AND
BROADWAY
in New Yo

HOUSE OF OLDIES

35 CARMINE ST. • NEW YORK, NY 10014

(212) 243-0500 • HOUSEOFOLDIES.COM

Life on the Flip Side

Bob Abramson handed the future to the other record stores, with predictably tragic results.

The other record stores went out of business.

While big chains were building big-box stores near big subway stops, Bob was minding his little shop on his little West Village street. While those stores were loading up on the latest audiocassettes and CDs, Bob was stocking the records he'd been stocking since the sixties.

Consequently, his House of Oldies has outlived monuments like Tower Records Lincoln Center, HMV Herald Square, and Virgin Megastore Times Square. Incidentally, Bob has since handed the future to the Internet, so you can expect that to be going out of business soon, too.

It's not that Bob doesn't like progress; it's just that he likes records. He started selling them in 1968 and he has had no reason to stop. He spends his days nestled among three-quarters of a million of them. "I love being here," he says. "It's either a sickness or a passion. I think it's a passion."

Here the latest hits, based on posted 45-rpm sleeves, include "Lonely Teenager" by Dion and "Surf City" by Jan and Dean. Here the top albums, based on posted LP covers, include *Here's Little Richard* and *Freddy Cannon's Solid Gold Hits!* Here you find Chuck Berry, Elvis Presley, the Beatles, the Stones, and Dylan—not to mention Frank Sinatra and Ella Fitzgerald—all on their original vinyl, leaning in bins and standing on shelves, just as they did before they were digitized, downloaded, and degraded.

The store spotlights rock 'n' roll, rhythm and blues, doo-wop, blues, soul, and pop, roughly from the forties through the seventies. It's not a garage sale, in that these records are not glazed with grape jelly or root beer. And it's not a garage sale, in that these records do not come three for a quarter.

It's also not a garage sale in that it's not a place for long browsing, since it has just one aisle, which gets blocked by just one browser. And that's a shame, since the store has dozens of those tempting record bins, and a wall of those tempting album covers and seven-inch record sleeves.

But you can spend some time admiring the other wall occupants, like the Everly Brothers, Bobby Darin, and the Eldorados. And that may help you know what you want—which may lead you to sticker shock. But Bob says that his prices shock only the people who don't understand.

He pulls out a copy of the Beatles' *Let It Be.* It is marked $90. He slips the disc out of its sleeve. It is shiny and flawless. "Show me where you're gonna find a first pressing of *Let It Be* that looks like that," he says. "It's a first edition. You're gonna pay for it."

Nevertheless, he has bargain bins, with LPs for $10. These are generally albums that are in more abundance or less demand. But like the ninety-dollar *Let It Be,* they are guaranteed. If you prefer the Motels to the Beatles, you go home an all-around winner.

The Motels aside, prime time here is the fifties and sixties, and most albums cost between $25 and $40. Even those prices can elicit comments like "Forty bucks for this? Are you serious?" Bob's reply: "Let me bring that to the attention of my buyer. It probably is too high."

The House of Oldies' record run started in 1962, when Richard Clothier opened it around the corner, on Bleecker Street. Bob became a customer. Then he became an employee. At twenty-four he became the owner. Richard didn't have the same passion.

Bob moved the store in 1980, when his landlord claimed that the fish store next door was taking over the space, though it never did. If not for that, he probably wouldn't have moved, just as he hasn't moved since. "I don't need to be the richest guy in the cemetery," he says.

As cassettes and CDs eclipsed vinyl, Bob put his famous sign in the window: NO CD'S/NO TAPES/JUST RECORDS. It seemed defiant, but Bob says it wasn't: "It was not to be elite. I did it 'cause the store was small, and I didn't want nine thousand people coming in here for CDs and tapes."

He may have had second thoughts (though probably not) ten years later, when the masses abandoned LPs for the alleged miracle discs. His aisle stayed clear while people rushed out to buy CDs of their records. He waited until they came back to buy records of their CDs.

Of course, whether they did or didn't, CDs (like cassettes) succumbed, and as they did, most of their retailers succumbed with them. House of Oldies has said farewell not only to HMV, Tower, and Virgin, but also to dozens of other record chains, record shops, and record departments.

Today its customers span generations, including the current generation of teens. "They'll come in and say, 'Got any Zeppelin on wax?'" Bob says. "They love the sound of vinyl on a decent system. It doesn't have to be a ten-thousand-dollar system. It can be a five-hundred-dollar system."

On his own system, incidentally, Bob plays mostly names like Dylan, Presley, and the Stones. "The greats are the greats because they're great," he says.

"Everybody thinks I have, like, secret albums that no one ever heard of. I don't. I don't have one album that you never heard of."

Food for Thought

*P*hilip Binioris knows that his cafe is the place for *dobos* and *Rigó Jancsi*. He's just not sure that it's the place for Google and Wikipedia.

This explains why a hangout for students from Columbia University has yet to connect those students to a new invention called the Internet.

That's not to say that it doesn't get in. There's a new invention called the smartphone, and many Columbia undergrads appear to be onto it. Philip can live with that. But he wonders whether the Hungarian Pastry Shop can live with a sea of laptops tainting its aura with Facebook and Twitter.

"I'm really afraid of it," Philip says. "People still talk to each other here. You really do have to think about it, because the place has been here for fifty years."

"People ask me what the magic of the pastry shop is. I think it's the interactive element. It's a strange balance that people create themselves in this space."

The point is that the Hungarian Pastry Shop is in good hands—which is reassuring, because it's also in new hands. Philip's been running it for two years. He's half the age of the shop. But he's perceptive enough to talk about it by using words like "magic."

The cafe is a place not only where cherry strudels get eaten, but where thoughts get discussed, ideas get sparked, and dissertations get written. It's a place where people can be alone together or together alone. And where they can take their time, in a world that seems to have so little to give.

It's a soothing yet stimulating room with walls of ivory and red, lined with mystical paintings that alternate with dimly glowing sconces. The paintings are the work of a former owner named Yanni Posnakoff, who at eighty is still contributing new art.

Among his old art are the cafe's handwritten menu signs, on which he was prescient enough not to include any prices. He did, however, include pastries that have since been lost. So people still order them. The shop embraces life with all of its disappointments.

But there is little disappointment in a place that greets you with cases filled with enough pastries to ease virtually any loss. Many of the recipes have been passed down from the Hungarian founders, and the selection has made the shop as much a tourist stop as a college lounge.

Choose from Sacher torte, Linzer tarts, hamantaschen, butterflies, Black Forest cake, and strudel, along with *dobos* ("white cake, rich chocolate icing, cooked caramel"), *Rigó Jancsi* ("bittersweet chocolate cream"), and *ishler* ("two hazelnut cookies with bittersweet chocolate cream"). There are éclairs, napoleons, Danishes, turnovers, cream puffs, and cream rolls. There are almond crescents, almond horns, almond bombes, and hazelnut slices. There are croissants, which surprisingly are the top seller, and there's baklava, because Philip's family is Greek.

Among the lost pastries are the Bullseye ("apricot/marzipan"), the Berliner ("nuts, raisins, rum, chocolate"), the Goosefoot ("cooked bittersweet chocolate, cherries"), and the Stephania ("hazelnut and chocolate"). You may want them because you can't have them. But their absence somehow mists them with a fascination that transports you to a bake shop long ago.

The original shop was founded in 1961 by Joseph Vecony, who ran it with his wife for fifteen years. It occupied just the front of the store. It was more for taking out than for staying in. Joseph didn't need an Internet connection, because he had no seats.

In 1976 Vecony sold the shop to Philip's father, Panagiotis Binioris, and his partners, Theodore "Ted" Maggos and Posnakoff. A decade earlier, Posnakoff had opened a nearby Greek restaurant called Symposium. Maggos had been a customer. Panagiotis had been a waiter and busboy.

Maggos designed the new layout, since he was a Columbia architecture professor. Posnakoff supplied the paintings and signs, since he was an artist. The partners later opened two restaurants; both have since closed, but Symposium is still run by Philip's uncle Christos Binioris, who once managed the pastry shop.

The shop has been blessed by its proximity to the Cathedral Church of St. John the Divine; it's a natural stop for the church's steady stream of visitors. Likewise, it has long appealed to Columbia students and staff. The bathroom walls boast intellectual graffiti.

In the nineties Posnakoff left to focus on his art, and Maggos died. Panagiotis (also known as Peter) ran the shop until 2011. Philip took over, but he is still frequently among family: His mother, Wendy, helps out, as do his three sisters, and Panagiotis makes rare appearances.

Philip wasn't new. He'd worked in the shop since he was thirteen. "It was the bedrock of my family," he says. "This was the foundation." He's partial to baking, he adds—"that, and conversations with some of the truly strange and unique characters that New York has to offer."

"One customer is in the process of trying to teach me ancient Greek," he says. "Mitchell Cohen is a good source of contemporary political argument. [Cohen's among the authors whose framed book covers hang on a wall.] You can sit down with anybody here and have a conversation and learn a lot."

Which brings him back to the Internet, which could change everything. "Who will it attract?" he wonders. "Who will it not attract?"

"Our customers get really, really upset with us when things aren't the way they expect them to be. . . . Things here happen very, very gradually. If they happen at all."

JJ HAT CENTER

310 FIFTH AVE. • NEW YORK, NY 10001
(212) 239-4368 • JJHATCENTER.COM

Still Keeping Your Head

You walk in and you believe it's a hat store from 1925, even though it's an IBM showroom from 1925. But it must have foreseen its destiny, or it wouldn't have waited till 1995 to house a hat store that opened in 1911.

In short, there's never been a tabulating-machine emporium that looked more like it should become a top-hat emporium. And that's part of why JJ Hat Center has become the last traditional spot in Manhattan to get the last thing that a fully dressed man puts on.

So, you acclimate to the marble fireplace, the oak woodwork, the terrazzo floors, the chandeliers, the friezes, and the gold leaf. And then you get acquainted with the fedoras, homburgs, toppers, trilbies, bowlers, berets, buckets, boaters, porkpies, and panamas.

And then you get assisted by an actual professional hatter, who keeps you from walking out of the place looking like Chico Marx.

"We've been selling only hats for a hundred years, through good times and bad," says Aida O'Toole, JJ's owner. "To me, it's amazing it has survived, to be honest with you. There were forty-eight men's hat stores just in Manhattan. We're the only true men's hat store left."

It is the hat store for any man who wants a hat—from Bruce Willis, the Hollywood movie star, to Bruce Gaylord, the Indianapolis stockbroker. "Our customers come from all walks of life," says Marc Williamson, JJ's manager. "We get everyone from construction workers to ambassadors."

They sell the best hat brands, at prices from $35 to $2,500, and they don't assume which end of that range the ambassador or the worker will be on. They stock hats by the thousands. They block hats, steam hats, and clean hats. And at least while they're on duty, the hat sellers wear hats.

"We developed a reputation in the city; people knew that we had all colors and all sizes, we were never out of anything, and when you walked through the door, you were a king." These are the words of Jack Lambert, the previous owner of the store, and the man who made it a survivor, according to the current owner.

It was in 1975, which was not the golden age of hats, that Jack, with his father, bought the fading business. He was confident that gentlemen's hats would rise again, which was understandable, because he'd been a hat man since he was in caps.

He is the son of a sales rep for Stetson, and he launched his career at his father's sales presentations, hanging model hats on racks. He became a stock boy for Worth & Worth, another of Manhattan's best hat stores. Then, for a while, he left the business for a career in marketing.

Meanwhile, JJ had been born in 1911, a block west on Herald Square, as part of a chain called Long's. Under its second owner, it became part of a Stetson-owned chain called Young's. Under its third owner, though, as Forstadt Hats, it found itself with headaches.

In midcentury a city street was a sea of fedoras. It seemed fitting that the first words in "Manhattan" were "man" and "hat." But in the sixties everything changed, especially men's heads. By the middle of the decade, hats were mostly off.

The stock culprit is John F. Kennedy because he didn't wear a hat to his inauguration, except that he did wear a hat to his inauguration. He went hatless thereafter, but historians and hatheads know that Kennedy was more sartorial effect than cause.

Hats were already on their way out in the fifties. (Eisenhower, too, went hatless, but no one seemed to notice.) "During World War II, men had steel pots on their heads for four, five years," Jack says. "When they came back, they didn't want to wear anything anymore."

By the mid-seventies men's hat stores were nearly a novelty. The one in Herald Square was showing its hard times. The Lamberts decided to save it. Since father and son were both John Joseph, they renamed it JJ. Then they set out to make it a destination.

Then they got lucky. In the eighties they had the cowboy-hat craze, the tweed-cap craze, the Indiana Jones hat craze, and the baseball-cap craze. They sold each of those hats by the thousands. But they continued to care for customers who still wanted hats that weren't a craze.

In 1986 Jack's father died, and about ten years later, the store had to move. Jack discovered the elegant site in the city's first sales building for International Business Machines. Except that it had long since stopped being elegant.

"They had covered the floor with hideous carpeting," Aida recalls. (Lambert says that they'd carpeted over carpeting.) "There was peeling paint, layers of it. The chandeliers were in the basement, and there was a drop ceiling. . . . I would never, ever, ever have pictured what [Jack] did with this place."

Aida, by then, was the manager, and soon after restoring the showroom, Jack joined a big hat company, and Aida took over. She honors the store's history with antique hatboxes, photos of the famously hatted (Bogey, Sinatra), and the neon Stetson sign that was over the front door.

She takes care not only of her customers but also of her non-customers. Anyone can come in and get a hat steamed and adjusted free. It is, of course, an enticement to become a customer—but it's also a sort of acknowledgment that hat people are a sort of club.

"This is the only place I've ever worked where customers are telling each other, 'Oh, you should take that one! It looks great!'" Aida says. "Hat wearers are more self-assured. They know there's got to be a time when a person feels good enough about himself to make his own choices."

TRADITIONAL & VEGAN
ITALIAN RESTAURANT

Meet an Old Flame

In the thirties, they lit a candle saluting the repeal of Prohibition.

They still have the candle.

They still light it each night.

They really liked repeal.

The candle is an agglomerate of eight decades of candles, so it is now less a candle than a wax mountain range. But they keep lighting it, because it's tradition, and few places have embraced tradition more than John's, which is traditionally known as John's of 12th Street.

Nick Sitnycky, an owner for forty years, makes preservationists look reckless. He could single-handedly make obsolescence obsolete. He refers to himself and his partner with words like "keepers" and "curators." The words fit: Everything they found in the place they have kept and curated.

This goes beyond the Italian recipes. It goes beyond the decor. It goes beyond the celebratory mound of white paraffin. They use a seven-foot-high air conditioner from 1950. They use a four-door refrigerator from 1919.

"Look at the way they used to make things," Nick says, admiring his fridge. "There was no planned obsolescence. They were built to last." He's right. The appliances work. Everything is cool. And preservation is unquestionably what has kept John's of 12th hot.

It begins, of course, with the recipes. John's serves Italian classics like veal scaloppine, eggplant alla Parmigiana, saltimbocca, and lasagna. But the old-time flavors are enhanced by the old-time atmosphere, which emanates from a dining room nearly unchanged for close to a century.

The lower walls are covered in marble slabs pressed in terrazzo. The upper walls are covered in paintings of scenes of Italy. "We paint," Nick says. "We paint between the marble and the murals. We paint the ceiling. Everything else, we feel we're the keepers of the museum."

"Everything else" includes the arched mirrors, the etched Florentine glass, the hand-carved sideboard, the marble pedestal, the Hammond clock, and the mahogany bar. And most strikingly, it includes the Belgian mosaic floor, whose tiles were laid one at a time, and which looks like carpeting.

The effect is soothing. This room has been cared for, so you sense that it will care for you. You can relax in it and have the food that it was built to serve. And you can have it for prices considerably below the ones you'd find for similar dishes in newer rooms.

John's seems to have had its patrons' convenience in mind from the start, or at least since the era whose demise it commemorates.

John was John Pucciatti, who arrived from Bevagna, Umbria, Italy, probably in the late 1890s, Nick says. He lived in the building and in 1908 opened the restaurant in what's now the front dining room. The two big booths that are there now are where the kitchen was then.

During Prohibition, John dutifully stopped serving liquor in the restaurant. Instead he served it in a room above the restaurant. "They'd say, 'You wanna have dessert upstairs?' You didn't have to have a code. You didn't have to say a password. They were two separate businesses, so the restaurant was not in jeopardy."

John's wife, known as Mama John, stocked the upstairs business, Nick says. "She was the brewmaster. She had a still in the backyard, making the hooch. And she made wine in the basement, in the dark. She may have had experience making wine in Italy."

After repeal, John added a dining room where the still had been. When it was completed, in 1938, he lit the first candle. Supposedly, it has been lit on every night of business since then. When the mound closes in on the ceiling, the staff whittles it down.

Clearly astute on many fronts, John bought his building. After the Second World War, he was joined in the business by his son, Danny. Nick, who had long loved the place, teamed up with a partner, Mike Alpert, to buy John's from Danny in 1972.

He lived in the neighborhood and had had his high school and college graduation parties here. "I was a stockbroker, and I had just gotten married," he says. "I turned to my good friend Mike and said, 'You wanna buy a restaurant?' You're in your twenties; you take a shot."

At first they were closed in summer, but then they opened in summer. At first they were closed on Mondays, but then they opened on Mondays. There were people, Nick says, who wanted to eat in summer and on Mondays, so he accommodated them. It was a good way to stay in business.

Another way was to add a vegan Italian menu, which they did a few years ago, to fleeting alarm. It paid off. Now a dietarily mixed couple can come in and have both chicken alla Rosa and seitan alla Rosa, which Nick believes they can hardly do anyplace else.

Vegan or not, you can enjoy a garden view in the back room. And in that room you can also enjoy the best view of the candle. Each afternoon at around 4:30, a waiter climbs up on a chair and ignites the currently available wicks, to usher in another festive night.

Nick is proud of all of it. He's glad he took the shot. But he somehow seems especially proud of his ancient appliances. He opens two doors of the antique refrigerator, revealing the cold beer and wine inside. "GE," he says, "should come and do a commercial."

KATZ'S DELICATESSEN

205 E. HOUSTON ST. • NEW YORK, NY 10002
(212) 254-2246 • KATZSDELICATESSEN.COM

The Meat Goes On

*K*atz's Delicatessen could sell tickets to get in.

Luckily, it gives the tickets away.

But you still have to take one to enter, and you have to return it to exit. If you don't, you can never leave, which would have its advantages.

Katz's preserves a lost tradition like no other place in New York. It's the tradition of the boisterous cafeteria that feels like home. It offers simple but succulent food at crowded but convivial tables. It's the Automat without the coin slots, knobs, and windows. Just the ticket.

Katz's also preserves the tradition of the Lower East Side Jewish deli, of which it was once one of dozens and is now one of one. For many New Yorkers it is headquarters for gastronomical essentials like pastrami, corned beef, salami, frankfurters, matzo ball soup, and kishke.

Among the old Jewish delis of Manhattan, including the Carnegie, Katz's is, at least in some ways, the most unassuming. Its sandwiches have no special names, unless you call "Katz's Pastrami" special. Its slogan is "A Delicatessen for 125 Years," though they change that every April.

It has walls with old photographs of stars like Dom DeLuise and old signs with observations like "Anytime is Cocktail Time." But it has looks and charm all its own, and those make it one of the old joints that many New Yorkers care about and accept just as it is.

You get your ticket at a little stand just inside the door, usually from a guy who doesn't seem inclined to discuss it. You're warned by signs that if you lose it, you'll owe at least $50. The signs don't mention imprisonment, but just in case, watch your ticket. You can be served by a waiter or pick up a tray, walk to food stations, and order direct; the ticket accommodates either option. Whichever you choose, your items are marked on the ticket, which is your check. The tickets are printed with prices from 50 cents to $4. Those are nostalgic.

If you want table service, you have to sit at the tables designated for table service. If you don't want table service, you have to sit at the tables not designated for table service. If you don't want table service, you have to search for the appropriate food stations. Katz's not only feeds you but also builds character.

Some people, intentionally or not, take their trays to the table-service tables. They run roughly a fifty-fifty chance of eviction. In the movie *When Harry Met Sally . . .* , Billy Crystal and Meg Ryan are served at a non-service table, but they had poetic license. (Their table is commemorated.)

Once you're settled at your table, whichever kind it is, you can take time to admire Katz's many relics. They include the tables themselves, the neon United States, and the dangling disc bearing the better-known slogan SEND A SALAMI TO YOUR BOY IN THE ARMY.

You can talk to strangers, and they'll probably talk back. You can feel lucky if you got hot dogs, because they're among the best in the city. And whatever you got, you can eat it without any shame, because everyone around you is eating the same thing.

Of course, the food's nutritional merits weren't much of an issue back when Katz's Deli and its competition were young. This was the cuisine of the Eastern European immigrants who arrived here by the millions from the late 1800s through the early 1900s.

Katz's reportedly began across the street on Ludlow in 1888 as Iceland Brothers, because it was begun by the Iceland brothers. The brothers weren't sure they could make it, so in 1903 they changed the name to Iceland & Katz, because they were joined by Willy Katz.

Vintage Spots: Lower East Side

KOSSAR'S BIALYS: EST. 1936

Bialys never became the stars that bagels did. But you can still get them by the bagful at the country's oldest bialy bakery. And that's about all you can do. It's a spartan place that speaks for itself, beyond a letterboard whose letters list the wares, and promise: WE GIV BAKERS DOZENS.

367 Grand St.; (212) 473-4810; kossarsbialys.com

RUSS & DAUGHTERS: EST. 1914

It's one of the last Jewish appetizing stores, and it may have been the first store to give billing to children who weren't sons. Thus, along with one of the city's most prized selections of smoked fish, it has one of the city's most distinctive old neon signs.

179 E. Houston St.; (212) 475-4880; russanddaughters.com

In 1910 Willy and his cousin Benny Katz bought out the brothers. According to legend, Benny hired a painter to make his new sign. The painter asked Benny what to paint on the sign. Benny snapped, "Katz's. That's all!" The painter painted: "Katz's. That's all." It became the deli's first slogan.

Another partner, Harry Tarowsky, joined up in 1917, around the time the store moved across the street because of subway construction. In the early years, Katz's became a meeting place for the community, including performers from the neighborhood's Yiddish theaters.

Willy Katz died, then Benny Katz and Harry Tarowsky died, and Katz's was passed along to Katz and Tarowsky descendants. In 1988 Martin Dell,

Vintage Spot: East Village

B&H DAIRY: EST. 1942

This kosher-dairy holdout still makes the likes of kasha varnishkes, even if it does spell them "kasha varniskas." At the counter, you can watch your food being cooked. At the tables, you're so close to the counter that if your menu is open, it's blocking the aisle.

127 Second Ave.; (212) 505-8065

his son Alan Dell, and his son-in-law Fred Austin joined in. Then they took over. Today the place is run by Alan's son Jake.

Among the deli's historical highlights is the coining of the salami slogan, when three sons of the owners were overseas in the Second World War. Another is the serving of Jewish food to six Gentile presidents: Roosevelt, Kennedy, Carter, Reagan, the first Bush, and Clinton.

And another is *When Harry Met Sally . . .* , because it has one of filmdom's best lines, which comes after Meg Ryan fakes carnal satisfaction at her table. Having witnessed the satisfaction, Estelle Reiner (the mother of the director, Rob Reiner) tells her server: "I'll have what she's having."

Alan Dell recalls several smaller but equally memorable moments. He recalls, for instance, a day near Christmas when his Jewish deli was filled with Santas. Similarly, he recalls a day when the pope was in town and his Jewish deli was filled with nuns.

He recalls a woman who sought him out to complain about his food. She showed him her rye bread and huffed, "Look at it. It has holes in it."

And he recalls a woman who sought him out to learn about his food. "She asked me, 'What is pastrami, anyway? Is that pork?'"

KEENS STEAKHOUSE

72 W. 36TH ST. • NEW YORK, NY 10018

(212) 947-3636 • KEENS.COM

The Pipes Are Calling

Big, fat juicy mutton chops, an enormous collection of smoking pipes, a library of single-malt scotches, and a giant painting of a naked lady. It's perfect for the whole family. If all the family members are men.

But Keens Steakhouse is also perfect for families with women and children, if they'd like a taste of New York with their baked Idaho. Of New York's oldest haunts, it is one of the most New Yorky. Yet after a century and a quarter, it's not always known to New Yorkers.

That's especially curious when you know that it's just around the corner from the Empire State Building, Madison Square Garden, and Macy's Herald Square. And it's even more curious when you see what it's hiding, which, besides its food, is a trove of treasures—including tens of thousands of long-stemmed clay pipes.

For all the sights—including the naked lady, who lounges above the bar and goes by the nickname of Miss Keens—the most compelling are those pipes, mounted in infinite rows on the ceilings, like a canopy guarding patrons against the intrusion of modern times. They are the pipes of the Keen's English Chop House pipe club, which dates to the days when the restaurant bore that name and apostrophe. It allowed members to keep a pipe on hand, primed for ignition. The pipes were numbered, stored by a pipe warden, and retrieved by pipe boys.

Among the members were Teddy Roosevelt, Albert Einstein, Babe Ruth, Enrico Caruso, Will Rogers, John Barrymore, and Buffalo Bill. The pipes of the famous are on display near the entrance—minus Einstein's, which, having been filched, is there in time but not in space.

It's amid this antiquity that patrons convene for sumptuous chophouse selections like Our Legendary Mutton Chop, even though it's now lamb. In 1950 James Beard wrote, "I am certain that at this point no other restaurant in New York exists where one may feast on such pedigree mutton chops as those at Keen's."

The feasting takes place in seven rooms on two floors in three conjoined town houses—each room with charms, and relics, of its own. There's the Main Bar, home to those scotches (close to three hundred) and to Miss Keens, whose presence recalls the time when Keens really was just for men. There's the Pub Room, which, with the Main Bar, can lose its serenity when celebrants pile in after the latest event at the Garden. There's the Lincoln Room, with what tradition holds is the program that the president was holding when he was fatally shot at Ford's Theatre. And there are the Lambs, Bull Moose, and Lillie Langtry Rooms, whose names command a brief review of Keens' eccentric history.

The place began as part of the Lambs Club, an enclave of the literary and the theatrical that migrated from London to Herald Square. The square at the time was home not only to its namesake newspaper, the *New York Herald,* but also to attractions more compelling than the Thanksgiving Day Shrek balloon.

It was a theater district, and the restaurant in the private club on the second floor inevitably became a draw for actors, playwrights, producers, and publishers. In 1885 its manager, Albert Keen, established Keen's English Chop House as an entity of its own.

The pipe club was another idea imported from England, where centuries earlier regulars kept their fragile clay pipes at their favorite taverns. At the club's height, Keens ordered thousands and thousands of the traditional churchwardens from the Netherlands.

"You'd come in and have your lunch or dinner," recalls Bill Ryden, a Keens regular for half a century, "and afterwards you'd present your card. They brought you your churchwarden clay pipe and a small bowl of tobacco. It was a different world."

Lifetime membership in the pipe club was about $5. When a member died, the pipe was saved, but the stem was broken. The club ended in the 1970s, but Keens has continued to bestow honorary club memberships on the likes of Liza Minnelli.

Which leads to Lillie Langtry, the actress and royal mistress who in 1905 was refused service because she was a woman. She sued the restaurant and won, then returned for a mutton chop. Keens commemorated the trauma by naming a room for the perpetrator.

The other room honoring a person is the Bull Moose Room, which honors Teddy Roosevelt, US president and, more important, New York City police commissioner. The Lambs Room, of course, is named for the club and decked with portraits of its illustrious if somewhat histrionic members.

That room and others are filled with framed photographs, Playbills, handbills, and newspaper pages recalling Keens' show-business roots. More keepsakes are in an alcove called the Herald Square Gallery. Only the Bull Moose Room, however, can claim its own moose head.

In 1977 an ailing Keens was rescued by the radiologist-restaurateur George Schwarz and his wife, the artist Kiki Kogelnik. They restored it and renamed it "Steakhouse," yet managed to keep it feeling like a private club where elegance is not equated with obsolescence.

One side of the awning still says "Chophouse," to comfort old-timers. But you don't have to be a regular to retreat to old times. "Our philosophy," says the longtime manager Bonnie Jenkins, "is that we're going to treat anyone who comes in like a guest in our home."

LA BONBONNIERE

28 EIGHTH AVE. • NEW YORK, NY 10014

(212) 741-9266

You Know Something's Cooking

*T*he aroma of La Bonbonniere will linger in your memory. Also in your coat, your shirt, and your pants. But you won't mind, after having one of the best breakfasts in New York City in one of the homiest hash houses in New York City.

La Bonbonniere is among the last of the cozy city diners at which you always know where your next meal is coming from. You're in the same room as the cook. You're in the same room as the grill. You're in the same room as decades of cooking on the grill.

But that's a good thing. For a while. La Bonbonniere could have a sign that says "Home Cooking," and it would be the truth. It's the luncheon-ette of your youth, if you're old enough to have had a luncheonette in your youth, and if you're not, it's the luncheonette of your youth.

It's not French. It is believed to have been owned by a French woman who was inspired by a 1920 poster for the Cabaret Bonbonnière. Her copy of that Walter Schnackenberg artwork still hangs on a wall. That makes a total of three French things: poster, fries, and toast.

But a *bonbonnière* is a candy store, which is a place full of treats, which is what this place is when you want treats like pancakes. There are good hamburgers, too, but La Bonbonniere is revered for its breakfasts. Every table has a pitcher of syrup on it. That's a clue.

Take a seat at, say, the window table beside the potted basil and the plastic lemons. Help yourself to one of the newspapers on the radiator under the pay phone. Look out at the people passing by who wish they were you. Then relax. And soak up the atmosphere.

You'll see beige metal walls festooned with things like the namesake poster, and postcards from Jamaica, Bangkok, the Philippines, and Abu Dhabi. Also clippings about celebrity patrons like Ethan Hawke and Molly Shannon, and numerous best-of citations, including one for "greasiest breakfast."

In front of the grill are a fake-white-marble Formica counter and six chrome-legged, maroon cracked-vinyl-topped stools. Above the grill are large panels of old marbled mirrors that don't do much reflecting because of all the atmosphere they have soaked up.

Your menu cover sports a happy chef who may or may not be French, and your menu, though omelet-heavy, sports the range of coffee-shop food. The selections are augmented by counter signs offering GUS'S HOME-MADE BOWL OF CHILI $6.50 and GUS'S RICE AND BEANS $7.00.

The exhaust fan is always humming; something is always sizzling. Before long, you are one with the bacon. And you come to accept that, especially once you are served, because you are served by people who care about you: Gus Maroulletis and Marina Arrieta.

Gus is the owner; Marina is the manager. They came here in the nineties after working together at the Mini Star diner in Queens. Before that, La Bonbonniere's history gets suitably hazy, but Gus has pieced it together probably as well as anyone.

There was a man who came in for breakfast into his late eighties, Gus says: "An Irish guy. We called him Yankees, because he wore a Yankees cap. He got bacon and eggs, juice, and coffee. He told me he used to come here in 1932, and they used to call it White Kitchen. Maybe it was white."

Yankees also told Gus that White Kitchen struggled in the Depression. He recalled that customers at the counter shared a coffee-stirring spoon. People would stir their coffee with it, then pass it along. It's not clear whether the tradition was continued by the French woman.

But theoretically, the French woman became the next owner, and she was followed by Charles Diratz, who was the owner for thirty-five years. Then came Gus and Marina, who could certainly have handled the place themselves but who nevertheless took on a third partner: Kitty.

Kitty, Marina says, was the diner's official hostess. She greeted people by rubbing their legs and jumping on their laps. She was a gray tabby. "Kitty was the star," Marina says. "She was like a dog. She used to say hi to everybody. She was a beautiful cat."

Beautiful to many patrons. Less beautiful to health inspectors, who seemed unschooled in the theory that pets can improve a person's health. So Kitty hid out during some inspections and got the place fined during others. But when fines escalated to threats of closure, Kitty was out of a job. She had worked about a dozen years. Friends who had taken her in for her retirement celebrated her eighteenth birthday in 2009. She made it to twenty. People still ask for her, and regulars still miss her. For some people, pancakes just taste better with a pussycat on your lap.

Marina and Gus are proud of their history. They point out their vintage trappings—the tin walls, the Toastmaster toasters, the TidyNap napkin dispensers. They especially treasure the old grill. Gus once replaced it with a new one. The new one was horrible. Everything stuck to it. He got back the old one.

The regulars like things that way, Gus says. "Customers don't like to change anything. They like old. They say, 'Please don't change anything.'" He would get another cat, in fact, if the inspectors would lighten up. "Everybody has cats and dogs around here, so what's the problem? I don't understand."

The Fountain of Youth

The Egg Malted, the Frosted Float, and the Creamsicle Freeze were among the things you could order from the old Lexington Candy Shop menu. Today, of course, to get bygone fountain drinks like that, you'd have to order them from the new Lexington Candy Shop menu. They're all there—the Egg Malted, the Egg Shake, the Frosted Float, the Malted Float, the Creamsicle Freeze, the Fresh Orange Freeze. They cost about forty times more than they did, but compare that to Manhattan rent. And considering how far back they can take you, eight bucks is not a bad fare.

Lexington Candy, which opened in 1925, is still equipped with its 1948 full-service soda fountain. Rather than waste it, the shop puts it to use preparing libations sadly unknown to generations schooled in McFlurrys, Blizzards, Frostys, and Fribbles.

The shop makes its frosteds—which is Old New York for milk shakes—with just milk, ice cream, and syrup. It makes its malteds with those three things plus actual malt powder. For its egg malteds and its egg shakes, it uses egg. For its Creamsicle Freezes, it uses fresh orange juice.

It makes its own fountain syrups, which it can add to a Coke to create the chocolate Coke, the vanilla Coke, the cherry Coke, and the lemon Coke. It mixes its sodas by hand, so it can use Coke syrup to make custom Cokes, not to mention the Coke-syrup-topped Coca-Cola Sundae.

It has ice-cream sodas, floats, lime rickeys, lemonade, and egg creams, but even with that iconic drink it dares to be different. A conventional egg cream is made with seltzer, Fox's U-bet chocolate syrup, and milk. Lexington uses its own syrup—and cream, though still no egg.

For such extreme behavior, Lexington Candy has gotten to keep its same corner store on the Upper East Side since the day it opened. It's still a neighborhood destination, but it's also an international destination. People come here for the fountain, but they also come for the shop.

It's about as close as a place can get to an old-time soda shop and still be open. It's close enough to have been used as a movie set, repeatedly. It reminds you that ice cream and soda can be things to relax over, rather than things to buy in disposable cups, carry out, and gulp while walking.

Lingering is what places like Lexington Candy were made for—and they were everywhere before lingering went out of style. As soda-dispensing machines developed through the nineteenth century, "soda fountain" became a term for a place to sip and socialize. That place at first was the drugstore, where at the time the druggist was free to create his own mysterious though allegedly life-enhancing potions.

Soon fountains were also a part of places like ice-cream parlors, luncheonettes, dime-store lunch counters, soda shops, malt shops, and candy stores. Lexington Candy Shop was among the candy stores—but just until its founders figured out that they could do better with food than with candy.

Soterios Philis and Tami Naskos, fresh from Greece, were the founders. They opened Lexington as just another corner soda fountain in the city. True to the name, they made candy. They sold their own chocolates—including Easter Bunnies—along with the era's popular brands.

In 1930 Soterios's son Peter came in from Greece and took a job at the shop, but not for long. Business got so bad in the Depression that the store couldn't support him. His father laid him off. He took a job at a fruit market. But in a couple years, he was rehired. Soterios waived the interview.

By 1948 Naskos was long gone, and Soterios and Peter had determined that there was more money in meals than in bunnies. Like other soda fountains, Lexington added breakfasts and lunches. Since then it's been a luncheonette. It just never changed its name.

In fact, it never changed much of anything, which is a major part of why it's one of the few fountains left pumping. Besides the fountain itself, it has its 1948 red counter and green-topped stools, its 1948 terrazzo floor, and its 1939 Hamilton Beach mixers.

In 1980 Peter's son, John, took over and continued the policy. He has carefully guided the store to its destination status. "Whenever we change things because we have to, we try to keep them close to the way they were," he says. "With time, people have come to appreciate it more and more."

It's a challenge. When he tried to replace the mixers, people were outraged. Now he takes the old ones to be repaired by "an old Mister Fix-it" in Queens. The Coca-Cola guys who come to fix the fountain, he says, "don't know how to do it. I have to tell them how to do it."

But it's worth it. Preserving the place has made it a favorite haunt of New Yorkers, including families who've been coming in through four generations. The 1925 menu is framed and hanging up for inspiration (though it hasn't helped John to recall what the Nabisco Sundae was).

Still, don't assume anything. While John will allow that his shakes are better than the ones at fast-food joints, he doesn't see those joints as the enemy.

"I happen to like McDonald's a lot; I happen to like Big Macs," he says. "Every so often, you gotta get a fix."

You Get What's Coming

*A*t Marchi's, if you order the fish they'll bring you the chicken, and if you order the chicken, they'll bring you the veal, and if you order the veal, they'll bring you the lasagna. And if you order the cabbage salad, they'll bring you the salami.

That's because, whatever you order, they'll bring you the salami, the cabbage salad, the lasagna, the veal, the chicken, and the fish—along with the fruit, the vegetables, the tossed salad, and the bread. And the crostoli. And a warm lemon fritter.

In short, they will bring you a five-course Northern Italian dinner—the same dinner they bring everybody, every night, every year. Marchi's has no menu. It's like a private eating club, and you're a member. Come in for the first time, and your waiter will bring you the usual.

You feel like you're in the Marchis' home, maybe because you are: The original dining room was once Lorenzo and Francesca Marchi's apartment. Lorenzo and Francesca are gone, but the restaurant is run by their sons, Mario, John, and Robert, and Mario's wife, Christine. Their dining room is abundantly homey, thanks to its red carpeting, white tablecloths, curtains, fireplace, and old paintings. And their dinner is consistently homey, since it's made from the same recipes that helped to make a restaurant out of a home.

You get to choose your drink, but after that, you just get. You first get warm bread and an antipasto centerpiece. It has honeydew, radishes, celery, tomatoes, and fennel, and is accompanied by Genoa salami and a platter of red-cabbage salad with tuna, better known as Lorenzo Salad.

This is the first course, which makes a fine meal. But it's followed by the second course, which makes another fine meal. It's a bowl of Lorenzo Lasagna, the restaurant's signature dish, which doesn't look like conventional lasagna but beats many lasagnas that do.

The third course is crunchy fried fish, served with green beans and beets; the fourth is roast chicken and roast veal, served with tossed salad and sautéed mushrooms. The fifth is dessert: a big bowl of fresh fruit, a slice of cheese, a warm lemon fritter, and a plate of crispy crostoli, which makes a fifth or sixth fine meal.

You get all of it (except for the drinks) for just over $50. About the only thing you don't get that you might want is butter. The Marchis keep it from you in order to keep you from eating too much bread and then not being able to eat everything else. These people have your back.

It all began with a hernia. Make that a double. It was a double hernia that led Lorenzo to become a chef, Mario says. He got the hernia doing construction work; then he got a bad operation. He decided to start searching for self-employment options.

Meanwhile, every night Francesca cooked dinner, the aroma of which was making Louis DeMarco crazy. Louis, a bachelor, lived upstairs and subsisted on cigars. He begged to partake of the Marchis' meals, at 50 cents a pop, which was a reasonable rate in 1929 for a restaurant that didn't exist.

Louis started bringing friends, and his friends started bringing friends, and before long Francesca and Lorenzo were living in a trattoria. For a while, Lorenzo still worked in construction and came home to work on his recipes, and Francesca still made Westinghouse lightbulbs and came home to cook for the neighborhood.

From the start they made one dinner, but they changed the dinner each night. They stopped changing during the Second World War because of the food shortages. After the war, they went back to changing. But by then it was too late. The regulars had taken to having one meal they could count on.

"They said, 'What the hell are you doing?'" Mario recalls. "It lasted only a year or two. They wanted what we had been doing, not what we were doing." The family agreed on one dinner that could last a lifetime. Now they've been serving it for about that long.

Back when the place was a hot spot, they served it to the likes of Sophia Loren, Joe DiMaggio, and Donald O'Connor. There are autograph books to prove it. The Marchi brothers also recall serving Marilyn Monroe and Arthur Miller, Nat King Cole, Grace Kelly, Charles Laughton, Toscanini, and Pavarotti. And Liberace.

After the war Lorenzo and Francesca bought the two buildings that housed their restaurant, always a key move to restaurant survival in New York. The Marchi family now owns ten buildings, and the restaurant has grown enough to have parts of itself reaching into nine of them. The parts include five dining rooms and an elegant outdoor dining garden with a stunning view of the Empire State Building. It's a spectacular place to eat, and yet it doesn't quite match the experience of having Lorenzo and Francesca's food while sitting in what was once their bedroom.

These days you can almost always sit in the original dining room, since business isn't what it used to be. But Marchi's still won't advertise. And it still won't put up a sign. It displays only a coat of arms. Christine says people peek in and ask, "Is this an embassy?"

Some neighborhood families came to the embassy for generations. But Marchi's now serves one of the great forgotten meals of Manhattan. And it's a meal that only improves once you get past the novelty, Mario points out: "By the fourth or fifth time, you really enjoy what's being put in front of you."

They Know the Score

Some people peek in and walk away. Some people run. They may have thought they wandered into a bohemian cocktail reception. They did. But what they didn't know was that they were invited. They had stumbled onto New York's merriest public sing-along.

They fled a dim basement that's the home of one of the city's bright spots: Marie's Crisis Café, which is no longer a cafe. It's a piano, a bar, a few stools, fewer tables, a two-foot stack of sheet music, and a regenerating crowd that sings show tunes for ten hours every night.

The crowd includes theater people and non-theater people, theater students and non-theater students, theater lovers and—well, other theater lovers. They sing alone or together, but most sing at the top of their voices. They sing songs from every show you've heard of and every show you haven't.

They can be daunting. After all, they're having fun without you. They seem like friends (many are); they seem to know all the songs (many do). But they're not thinking about you. They're busy. They hardly notice if you come in. They don't stand you on a chair and make you belt out all of *Oklahoma!*

If you want to belt, on the other hand, your opportunities can run from "They Say It's Wonderful" (*Annie Get Your Gun*) to "Let the Sunshine In" (*Hair*). Often, you can belt out most of the original cast album. Once the crowd sings "Little Shop of Horrors," it's usually on its way to "Suddenly Seymour."

The exuberant chorus nearly transforms the bar into a Broadway stage, which is impressive, considering what the place actually looks like. Backing the bar is a dusty antique mirror etched with revolutionary war scenes. That's the highlight. There's not a whole lot more to sing about.

The decor is a medley of ceiling beams, floor planks, lines of Christmas lights, and at least five different kinds of wall paneling. An alcove holds a bench topped with a gouged-out red seat pad. Built into a wall are a dead fireplace and a dead tube TV that even when it lived was turned on only for the Tony Awards.

But between the television and the fireplace stands a Kawai console upright, retrofitted with red plastic counters from 1972. And behind the piano sits the life of the party: the upright piano player. He plays, he sings, he cracks wise, and he always knows one more song than the crowd.

The king of the keyboardists is Jim Allen, so crowned because he's been at Marie's for about twenty-five years. The sheet music is stacked beside him, but he rarely touches it. He memorizes. He claims he has about fifteen thousand songs in his memory.

He sees Marie's as a survivor, which makes it a good match for lots of patrons. "I always compare it to a rathskeller in Germany during World War II," he says. "People come in here and sing like there's no tomorrow. Nobody seems to care what's going on outside in the world."

Thus, to the role of performer he's added that of preservationist. He works hard to keep the music coming and the singers singing. He has his limits. That explains the faded spot on the wall behind him. It's where, when he reaches his limit, he starts banging the back of his head.

"I got a request for *Annie, Grease,* and *The Sound of Music,*" he recalls. "An hour later, I got the same request. I just started hitting my head. . . . I love *Chicago,* but 'All That Jazz' I've played literally over ten thousand times. With *Chicago,* people only know 'All That Jazz.'"

He tries to shepherd the novices to new pastures, he says: "My philosophy is to play nine songs they know and one song they don't know." It's apparently worth the trouble, not only for the sake of his head, but also for the sake of a little place that holds a lot of history.

The bar's location was famous before it was the bar's location. It was the site of the house in which Thomas Paine died in 1809. The founding father was the author of the Revolutionary War pamphlet series "The American Crisis," which begins with the line "These are the times that try men's souls."

Around 1925 the current building was purchased by Marie Dumont. She called it her cafe because she served food. And she called it her crisis in honor of the man who helped to establish a country where people would be free to request songs from *The Lion King.*

Jim, who in his quarter century has compiled some Marie's history, says the bar moved through phases including one as a jazz club. It was in '72, he says, that it became a piano bar. It was one of several in the area, including the lamented nearby Five Oaks.

Before long it was not just a piano bar but a Broadway piano bar. That focus, Jim is certain, is what has kept Marie's a survivor. Other piano bars let you sing anything. But people need more structure: "If Marie's ever loses its identity, we'll go the way of Rose's Turn and Danny's Skylight."

Accordingly, Jim is armed with showpieces for diversion. Among them are his medleys for many occasions. "I have the Maudlin Medley, the Prostitute Medley, the Richard Rodgers Waltz Medley," he says. "That one makes the room really shine for twelve minutes."

He has to protect the identity. He has to protect his head. "If someone comes in here and hears Bon Jovi, they're gonna request other Bon Jovi," he says. "Once you've broken the seal, you have no reason to say 'I can't play that.' There used to be a Tori Amos book here. I threw that out."

MCSORLEY'S OLD ALE HOUSE

15 E. SEVENTH ST. • NEW YORK, NY 10003

(212) 473-9148 • MCSORLEYSNEWYORK.COM

There's Not Much Choice

*L*ife was simpler in 1854, and McSorley's has made it its business to keep it that way. It's still serving basically one drink. It's still serving that drink in one place. Not so long ago, it was still serving the drink to one sex. Maybe that's why the bar still has appeal to young and old. To the old, simplicity's a comfort. To the young, it's a novelty.

At a glance, McSorley's is another old bar with a lot of old stuff on the walls, typically so packed with revelers that you can't see the stuff if you want to. But there's a difference. There's an authenticity. For one thing, it really is old. For another thing, it acts like it really is old.

It does indeed sell one hard drink: McSorley's Ale, in light or dark. It has a coal-burning stove, sawdust on the floor, and no stools at the bar. Its most famous dish, outside of burgers, is cheese with onions and crackers. You pay cash, which is put in soup bowls. There has never been a register.

But there are gas lamps, and an icebox, and wood barrels out front, and that requisite of former men's bars, a picture of a naked lady. There are huge century-old urinals that are worth fighting the crowd to get to, and there's an egalitarian slogan: "Be good or be gone."

"There's tremendous atmosphere here," says Matthew Maher, who is fairly authentic himself, having owned the bar since 1977. "John Lennon had the best quote of anybody. He said McSorley's is a place of history, mystery, and mysticism. That summed it up for me. That's what I'd say about the place."

Vintage Spot: Soho

Fanelli Cafe: est. 1847

It wasn't Fanelli until the twentieth century, but it appears to have been at least a sort of a bar in the nineteenth. Regardless, it's warm and inviting, and it's indisputably on its way to becoming the only place in its neighborhood with any age to speak of at all.

94 Prince St.; (212) 226-9412

That said, he gives credit where at least some is due: "I think the glass of ale has a lot to do with it. It's a delicious glass of ale. It's fresh, and there's no preservatives in it. And there's no hangover. You never see anybody here with a hangover. You can't drink that much of it, because you get full."

"Women love that glass of ale," he adds. "I didn't think they would, but they do."

It's a good thing that they love it. They waited 116 years to have it.

McSorley's was designed to be old from the time it was new. Its original name, in 1854, was The Old House at Home. It was named for a pub in Ireland by a man who had left Ireland to start a pub here. His name was John McSorley. He's referred to as Old John.

John's first son was Peter, but it was his later son Bill who would guide the bar into the second of its first three centuries. Peter was immortalized elsewhere. In 1882 there was a play on Broadway called *McSorley's Inflation.* In it, the bar owner's name was Peter McSorley.

Bill took over after Old John died in 1910. By then the bar's course had been more or less set. John had bought the building, and he had tried

Vintage Spot: Nolita

MILANO'S BAR: EST. 1923

As with many old bars, Milano's year of birth is negotiable, which is often more than you can say for Milano's itself. In a crowd, you can barely squeeze between the barstools and the wall. But that hasn't kept the place from becoming one of the longest-lasting of the old neighborhood bars.

51 E. Houston St.; (212) 226-8844

selling liquor. The bar paid its last rent in 1888 and poured its last booze in 1906.

It officially become McSorley's around the turn of the century, when the Old House sign fell and had to be replaced. The new sign read "McSorley's Old Time Ale House." Eventually the bar became Timeless, but it has always stayed Old.

It sailed through Prohibition with neither a raid nor a secret password. Some say it's because whatever it was selling was not exactly beer. Yet the bar ended up in the hands of a cop. In 1936 Bill sold it to his cousin Daniel O'Connell, whom it inspired to leave the NYPD.

O'Connell died three years later and left the bar to his daughter, who became the first and only owner who wasn't allowed in. McSorley's was still men-only, so Dorothy O'Connell Kirwan made her husband, Harry, the manager and entered her place only after closing on Sundays.

In 1940 *The New Yorker* ran a piece about the bar by the beloved city chronicler Joseph Mitchell. The piece was called "The Old House at Home." It was a milestone for McSorley's in a way that articles decades later would be for the Carnegie Delicatessen and the Four Seasons restaurant.

In 1964 Matthew Maher was about to become a sheep farmer in Australia. At the time, however, he was still a van driver for a meat company in Ireland. While transporting sausages near Dublin, he saw a disabled vehicle. He picked up its owner. The owner was Harry Kirwan.

Harry ended up tagging along with Matthew for the rest of the week. He offered him a job at McSorley's, where a cousin of Matthew's worked. Matthew abandoned the sausages and transported himself to New York. He has yet to get back to the sheep in Australia.

In 1969 McSorley's got sued for not letting women in. So in 1970, it let women in. The Kirwans' son Danny, now in charge, wanted the first woman served to be Dorothy. She declined. She had promised her father that she would keep out, and she kept her promise.

There were many who thought that McSorley's would never be the same, and, of course, they were right. But they weren't right if they thought McSorley's wouldn't survive. Matthew was sure that it would, and in 1977—when he'd saved enough money—he bought it from Danny Kirwan.

He even installed a ladies' room (though it took him about ten years), not to mention two daughters, who work at the bar. But that's about it. "You can't interfere with what's there," he says. "You don't even want to take a piece of wood out, 'cause the atmosphere goes with it."

To fully savor the atmosphere, it's wise to visit early. Later, so many people can cram in that a guy has to keep some out.

Matthew knows that the scene can be challenging. But that challenge, he says, can be met. "You can't enjoy McSorley's," he says, "until you roll with the rhythm."

MUSIC INN WORLD INSTRUMENTS

169 W. FOURTH ST. • NEW YORK, NY 10014

(212) 243-5715 • MUSICINNWORLDINSTRUMENTS.COM

Still Making Noise

Jeff Slatnick would never bump his head on a dangling balalaika, but that doesn't mean he can never get beaned by a plummeting bulbul tarang. And in fact he did, but only because it was on the saxophone case he was leaning against while sitting on the floor talking to a woman about the banjoleles.

A bulbul tarang is an Indian banjo, a banjolele is a banjo ukulele, and Jeff Slatnick can play both, since he can play everything—which he seems to have in stock, which is why the initial challenge of Music Inn World Instruments is to find the best way to fit in.

It's a profusion of exotic instruments, less displayed than clustered, and barely contained by obscured structures that you presume to be walls. It's where instruments piled on the floor merge with instruments suspended from the ceiling such that you fear that if one is extracted, all of Greenwich Village might collapse.

But enough of them have been extracted to keep the store resonant for decades, while most other Village haunts of the folk era have gone silent. In another time, they were extracted by the likes of Bob Dylan and John Lennon. But the proprietor isn't sitting around waiting for either to come back.

Jeff sends sitars and psalteries all over the world, while equipping locals with everyday needs like Portuguese guitars and washboards. At a typical moment, he's selling a Jew's harp to one guy and a toy piano to another. Spend some time in this place and you think that charangos are the latest thing.

Jeff also builds and repairs instruments in his basement workshop, where he retreats to play his current favorite, the electric sarod. It's an otherworldly creation, evolved from the Indian original, which sounds like digital bagpipes. It puts him in a near-hypnotic state.

Maybe that's just what you need after decades at work in a place that leaves congas, maracas, tambourines, and bells within easy reach. All day long, people grab things and make noises that may or may not have been intended to come from the instruments they've decided they can play.

But Music Inn thrives on spontaneity and surprise. No fan of chain stores, Jeff wouldn't want you to mistake his place for one.

You know this out on the sidewalk, where you see window displays with record albums like *Banjo Music of the Southern Appalachians* and *The Belle of New York starring Fred Astaire.* And you know it heading in, when you see the store hours on the door: MONDAY THRU SATURDAY/ SOMETIME BEFORE 12 P.M. TO SOMETIME AFTER 6:30 P.M.

You might catch the harmonica guy playing just outside the door, but turn right and you'll see the hubcaps hanging just inside the door. The rest of the main floor contains the non-percussion instruments, along with a cash register that looks like it rang up a century.

To the left you'll notice a staircase, which, if not congested, will take you down to see the many pleasures of the cellar. They include the percussion instruments, along with old records and tapes, an Edison phonograph, and books like *Art of Northwest New Guinea.*

At the center of it all is Jeff, who at a given moment could be playing, demonstrating, carving, repairing, or slurping down take-out noodles. If you think that he's the sixtyish guy with the tousled gray hair, the bushy gray beard, and the owlish tortoiseshell glasses, you're right.

But if you think he's stuck in the sixties, you're wrong. The sixties gave him Eastern philosophy, which prescribes living here and now. For sure, many of his customers are children of the sixties, but at least as many are the children of the children of children of the sixties.

"When people say to me, 'I miss the good old days; you didn't have to lock your door,' I say, 'Yeah—and black people couldn't drink from the water fountain,'" he says. "I have memories of the Village," he adds, but to that he further adds, "Don't waste too much energy judging the world's evolution."

Indeed, though it's hard to tell, Music Inn itself has evolved.

The store was opened in 1958 by Jerry Halpern, who named it Music Inn because it was a record shop. The cubbyholes on the walls that were later crammed with toy drums, zithers, and tumbis were installed to hold the latest hits by Bobby Darin, Chuck Berry, and Elvis.

It was a hopping place. But Jerry was a mercurial man. He always loved other cultures, and those cultures found their way to the shop. Musical instruments systematically stole space from recorded music, and by 1962 the store was Music Inn World Instruments.

Jeff first worked for Jerry in 1967. He had come from a musical family and was playing sitar in clubs and commercials. He left the store after three months to move to California, where he studied sarod for nine years with the master Ali Akbar Khan.

But he returned in 1976 and settled in at the store (while playing occasional gigs in restaurants). He evolved from employee to manager to owner. Jerry died in 2010. Jeff has taken his place as the proprietor you're a little afraid of.

Jeff confirms the legends. Yes, Dylan lived a couple doors down in the sixties and came in to browse. Yes, Lennon dropped by, too. Yes, to discourage dilettantes, Jerry put up a chain and charged people a dollar to enter. Jeff approved, but he hasn't continued the policy.

He's more concerned with the present, and he doesn't love all of it. The chain stores, he says, are "just a way for some guy to sit on a beach. It's no way to run a music store." Nor is the Internet, he adds: "Now I have to compete with some guy who's sitting in his bathrobe in Toledo, Ohio."

NATIVE LEATHER

203 BLEECKER ST. • NEW YORK, NY 10012

(212) 614-3254

The Sum of Its Parts

One reason that Native Leather is still around is that the horse stores aren't. Not that it captured the horse business. It just captured the horse buckles.

When city saddleries threw in the towel, you could go for the brass ring, explains Dick Whalen, one of the founders of the store. "They sold their buckles by weight for scrap. You could get a pound of brass buckles for half a buck. I stockpiled buckles. I still have buckles I bought in the sixties."

So you can buy a twenty-first-century belt with a twentieth-century buckle, but after all, a buckle's a buckle, and it doesn't know you're not a horse. Bits and pieces from the past, in bags and boxes on the floor, are part and parcel of what makes Native Leather a Greenwich Village survivor.

It's also a Greenwich Village challenge, because it has no qualms about stuffing itself with merchandise until you can barely get to it. Native Leather is a jungle of belts, jackets, coats, vests, wallets, hats, bags, gloves—and sandals, which are displayed on gruesome false feet.

The store is run by Carol Walsh, who took over in the nineties, but Dick still works the sales floor and still makes bespoke sandals. Their hippie-esque vibe propitiously appeals to shoppers across generations, but it also belies their business sense, which has repeatedly saved the joint's hide.

In the mid-sixties, Dick says, there were eighteen leather shops in the Village. By 1979 nearly all of them were gone. But the next year he doubled the size of his store. He says that he just had the best leather. But he acknowledges that he cared enough to go out and bag bargain buckles.

"I was probably the only guy in the business buying with the future in mind," he says. "Most of the others didn't take the long view. They were guys on summer break from college who were gonna do this till they were bored with it. I bought long-term. And I scrounged a lot."

The store arose from scrounging, though not exclusively Dick's. It boasts a classic Greenwich Village bohemian beginning. In a way, it began with Allan Block, a Midwestern violinist who in the fifties came to the Village and opened a leather shop on MacDougal Street.

Block—the father of the blues singer Rory Block—eventually moved his store to West Fourth Street. There, Allan Block Sandal Shop became known not only for its sandals but also for its weekend jams with local, and often rising, folk musicians.

Block hired Bruce Britton, who Dick says opened his own shop while on probation for swiping a motorcycle. His shop was on Thompson Street, then in a basement on MacDougal, which he could have called The Leather Shop but instead called The Britton Shop.

In 1961, Dick says, after two years on MacDougal, Britton decided he'd rather become a carpenter. He persuaded his employee Ken Martin to take over the store. In 1962 Dick's girlfriend bought sandals from Martin. Dick liked the looks of them.

That year he took his NYU business education down to the basement and started making sandals himself. He enjoyed it, thanks in part to his work in bomb disposal in Korea: "That set you up," he says. "Whatever you were gonna do in life couldn't be as bad as that."

He and Martin became partners, but Martin had the less business-friendly education of a literature major. Dick says that Martin kept the business records in a big trash box. He was not an ideal fit. Dick was the store's best hope.

By '63 the store had moved up to an efficiency on Sullivan Street. "It became a hangout," Dick says. "There were other craftsmen on the street.

We'd chip in and all eat dinner there." By '64 Britton was in San Francisco, Martin was in Utica, and Dick owned The Britton Shop.

He went on to open Britton Shops on St. Mark's Place and Greenwich Avenue, and briefly up in Woodstock, Hyannis, and Provincetown. In 1969 he moved the first shop to its current home on Bleecker Street. By 1971, he says, "I couldn't look at leather anymore."

His retail future, he discovered, was in less instead of more. He abandoned all the stores, plus a workshop on Crosby Street. In 1972 he reopened the Bleecker Street shop under the name of Natural Leather and decided to make just that one store count.

That's why he expanded it in 1980. And that's why he hired Carol in 1983. Together they braved irritations like the running-shoe revolution, and managed to keep the store in the present while charmingly in the past.

Carol bought the store in 1994, and Dick came with it. He's there five days a week, clad in sandals from March through November. Along with sandals, he makes belts, and he does leather repairs. And though he comes across as tough as leather, he has his supple moments.

"A guy brought in sandals from 1969 from the St. Mark's store," he recalls. "I looked at them and said, 'They're a little old.' He said, 'They're the only things I have from that time of my life that I still use.' I fixed 'em. He put me in a bad spot. I though he was gonna break out in tears."

In short, he loves the place. So does Carol. But she acknowledges that she saddled it with an unforeseen challenge when she renamed it.

She used the old logo, so locals hardly noticed. But others see "Native Leather," she says, "and they come in looking for headdresses."

"I have Navajo belt buckles. I have Zuni belt buckles. I have Hopi belt buckles," she says. "But that's not because it's called Native Leather. It's because we sell belt buckles."

Unextreme Makeover

Wally Tang said his nephew could fix up the place to look sleek, cool, and trendy. That nearly killed the deal. The nephew told his uncle that he'd fix up the place to look like itself. That's why Nom Wah is still around.

It was a generational aberration, and it led to a new life for an old haunt in the heart of Chinatown. Now New York City still has its beloved Nom Wah Tea Parlor, and Wilson Tang, Wally Tang's nephew, has a seventy-hour workweek.

He is dedicated to running the restaurant that was possibly the first, and is probably the oldest, to serve dim sum in New York. He has been hailed as a hero for rescuing and redoing the place. He cops to the rescue. He demurs on the redo.

"People tell me what a great job I did on the renovation," he says. "I didn't do anything. This is your classic less-is-more." He did remake the kitchen, install new lights, and patch and paint. But Nom Wah still looks so last century. Wilson left old enough alone.

Nom Wah charms you with its guileless hand-lettered sign, then cheers you with its cherry-red booths and lemon-yellow walls. It transports you with its wooden hutch holding rows of antique tea tins, and with relics including its fountain stools and its retired Chambers stove.

Settle in for dim sum, the Chinese snacks that are commonly served for brunch and lunch but at Nom Wah are served all day. The stars of the

Vintage Spot: Tribeca

Fountain Pen Hospital: est. 1946

They're all here—your Parkers, your Sheaffers, your Montblancs, and your Watermans, in "the world's largest inventory of vintage fountain pens." As the name suggests, your old pens can be nursed back to health. Then again, you could always break down and buy a ballpoint.

10 Warren St.; (212) 964-0580; fountainpenhospital.com

menu—which have stars on the menu—include the roast pork bun, the shrimp and snow pea leaf dumplings, and the "original" egg roll.

For the novice, it's an exploration; for the regular, it's a comfort. Either way, it's tasty food with six condiments on each table. Some places serve dim sum from carts, but here you get a checklist and a waiter who will help you determine whether your best bet is the fried shrimp ball.

It wasn't like this a few years ago. After sixty years in the business, Wally Tang had sort of let Nom Wah go, Wilson says. It was less a restaurant than a social club; it was in the sights of the health department; and it was more or less on the death watch of city chroniclers.

Wilson, meanwhile, was in finance. He had worked for Morgan Stanley and ING Direct, though in between he had run a bakery on the Lower East Side. Wally Tang guessed that he could get his nephew to take over the tea parlor if he let Wilson turn the tea parlor into a scene.

Wally took Wilson to Red Egg, a dim-sum palace on nearby Centre Street that had mirrors and curtains and light balls and at night was a party. "He wanted to entice me," Wilson says. "He said, 'You can make it hip.' I was like, 'I could care less. I like it just the way it is.'"

This was probably a relief to Wally, who must have liked it the way it was, too, since he had barely changed anything in it since 1974. In 2011 Wilson took over Nom Wah, lightly spruced it up, and got congratulated both for making it over and for leaving it alone.

It was a comeback worthy of a place that's been a survivor from the start. When Nom Wah first appeared, Chinatown was still the scene of tong wars. The quaint bend in Doyers Street got the nickname Bloody Angle, in a nod to its convenience for gangland hatchet murders.

In 1920 Po Yu Choy opened Nom Wah right at the bend, at 15 Doyers. It reputedly served dim sum and tea from the start. Apparently at some point it also had a soda fountain, since an undated photo shows a neon Nom Wah sign that says SODA FOUNTAIN.

Under the Choy family, Nom Wah grew to include a bakery. In 1968 it moved next door, to 13 Doyers. But in 1950 the Choys, wittingly or unwittingly, had secured Nom Wah's future by giving a first job to a sixteen-year-old immigrant named Wally Tang.

Wally worked hard enough to work his way up to manager and then, in 1974, to owner. He did his own part to secure the future first by buying Nom Wah's building and later on by employing Wilson, whether Wilson wanted employment or not.

Wilson's interest grew along with his finance career. "I always had that entrepreneurial side," he says. "I dictate my own future here. I was always working for the man. Here, I'm the man. How well I do is up to me."

Since becoming the man, he's been finding out just how true that is. "What I do on a daily basis is a lot of work," he says. Food bloggers tend to cast him as a celebrity, he adds: "I'm like, you have no idea how hard it is. But thanks for glamorizing my life."

With or without fame, he says, Nom Wah will stay simple. His plans for expansion don't reach much beyond a food truck.

"I want to keep true to our mission," he says. "Once we start selling lobsters and all this crazy stuff, then I've gone too far."

OLD TOWN BAR

45 E. 18TH ST. • NEW YORK, NY 10003

(212) 529-6732 • OLDTOWNBAR.COM

Don't Make a Scene

The Old Town Bar doesn't have the city's biggest TV screen. It does, however, have some of the city's biggest urinals. Oddly enough, these facts sum up the bar's unique attraction. It invites you to relax and celebrate life's old-fashioned pleasures.

Old Town has a nice antique bar, but many bars have a nice antique bar. Old Town has good burgers and fries, but many bars have good burgers and fries. What Old Town has that others haven't is what it doesn't have. It doesn't have a big head. And its name means what it says.

"We try to treat everyone normally," says Gerard Meagher, one of the owners and the general manager. "We don't want to be a hip place. We want to be a normal place. People can blend in here. We treat everybody the same until they show that they don't deserve it."

Of course, antihip can be hip. But Gerard isn't worried. If hipness managed to sneak in, he says, Old Town wouldn't recognize it. "New York has a reputation for attitude. We try to stay away from it. Even if we tried to do it, we wouldn't be able to do it properly."

What they do properly is run a civilized saloon from 1892, where people can eat, drink, and be merry almost the way people did then. Old Town frowns on cell phones. It displays framed book jackets. It has just one television set, and that's not always on.

"Having a lot of TVs, you sort of chase out the people who aren't interested," Gerard says. "We're more conversational. People can talk to each other as opposed to staring at a TV screen." He acknowledges that "there's a big market" for multiple TV screens but adds that "there's also a market for people not interested in that."

He's even more radical on sports, which is mostly what's on bar TVs: "People don't come to New York because there are good sports teams. People come to New York because it's an artistic environment, a cultural environment. We cater to those people. We don't shun the sports people, but there's a lot more to life than sports."

Needless to say, there are many who disagree. They're welcome anyway, but clearly Old Town can survive without them. It favors the New Yorkers who know and care about New York. After all, it has gone out of its way to preserve its pieces of it.

The centerpiece is the original 55-foot mahogany-and-marble bar backed by the 258-square-foot beveled mirror. Across from the bar are booths with genuinely distressed wood tables, and benches whose seats swing open for hiding drinks during Prohibition.

The tile floor is also original, as is the tin ceiling, except for its color, which you might call legendary-brown. It was last painted white in 1952 on Election Day (bars were once closed that day). The brown is tobacco smoke. It's a nice brown. But don't try this at home.

Among the wall hangings is a framed menu from December 11, 1937. The selections that night included fried calf's liver with onions, and larded saddle of hare, sour cream sauce, buttered noodles, and red cabbage. These days you can hardly ever get your saddle larded.

Old Town has converted gas fixtures. It has chrome cash registers. It has a dumbwaiter, which is still used to bring you food. But the most celebrated of its furnishings are the two still reserved for men, just as the bar itself was once: the Great Hinsdale Urinals.

They rise several feet from the floor. They are practically walk-ins. They say: "The Hinsdale Patent Nov. 1 1910." They were given a centennial party on November 1, 2010. It included a champagne toast and a viewing for curious and daring women.

Perhaps anticipating this gala in 1892, Old Town set the stage for the event by getting itself launched. It started life as a German restaurant and bar by the name of Viemeister's, then apparently held other German names including L.E. Reichenecker Café.

In time for Prohibition, it became a speakeasy called Craig's Restaurant. In time for repeal, in 1933, Claus Lohden renamed it Old Town. Twenty years later, after Claus died, his son Henry took over. When Henry died, his wife, Bernice, took over, along with Gerard's father, Larry Meagher.

Gerard took charge in the nineties, with his father as "guiding force." Larry Meagher died in 2008. The bar is now owned by Gerard, his two brothers, and his two sisters. They also own the building, which ensures that Old Town can keep getting older.

Since the bar is a natural stage set, it has starred in movies and TV shows; for years it appeared in the opening of NBC's *Late Night with David Letterman.* But it has stayed humble. "That's what it's all about," Gerard says. "People come in here and feel comfortable. They don't feel out of place."

But they can still get a lift—particularly in the men's room. At least, that's what Gerard suggested at an earlier party for his urinals. Speaking to the *New York Observer,* he observed of the porcelain monuments, "They make a man feel more important than he actually is."

P.J. CLARKE'S

915 THIRD AVE. • NEW YORK, NY 10022

(212) 317-1616 • PJCLARKES.COM

The Storied Saloon

There's special value to a bar that's managed to get itself connected to the greatest things in popular culture having to do with bars. P.J. Clarke's is the bar where Johnny Mercer wrote "One for My Baby," the greatest song having to do with bars. P.J. Clarke's is the bar that was called Nat's Bar in *The Lost Weekend,* the greatest movie having to do with bars. P.J. Clarke's is the bar with a permanent table for Frank Sinatra, the greatest saloon singer who ever lived. Or so Clarke's claims. And so it's become the bar of grand allusions—the bar that people conjure up when they conjure up a bar.

Naturally, it also has claims that have nothing to do with bars, and it relishes those every bit as much as the others. Here's where Buddy Holly proposed; here's where Jackie took John Jr. and Caroline for lunch; here's where Dick Clark came to chill out after he rocked the new year in.

Here's where Ted Kennedy came to feel better after losing the nomination to Carter, and here's where you can come to feel better, too. Start by noticing that the bar is a brick box in a skyscraper canyon. Then enter the box and take a moment or two to notice what you've entered.

It's two rooms of old brick, old wood, old tiles, and old glass (stained and etched), with old doors, old clocks, old mirrors, and old cash registers (all retired). You may get lurched into the present by the TV or the meze plate, but there's enough to quickly lull you back to more placid times.

Vintage Spot: Midtown East

LA GRENOUILLE: EST. 1962

This cozy spot in a cozy town house is bedecked with chandeliers, paintings, sconces, crystals, and luxuriant bouquets. It's also the last of the great Midtown French restaurants. As such, for many it is an indulgence. But at least it makes you feel indulged.

3 E. 52nd St.; (212) 752-1495; la-grenouille.com

Vintage Spot: Upper East Side

SUBWAY INN: EST. 1937

There's a subway entrance to its left and a Subway restaurant to its right, making it part of what's likely the only spot in New York with three different subways. More important, it's one of the city's most treasured dive bars and boasts some of the city's most worn-out Formica tables.

143 E. 60th St.; (212) 752-6500

You can still sit at a table with a red-and-white tablecloth; you can still get a Coke, if that's what you want, in a little Coke bottle. You can still hear Nat King Cole, who called the bacon cheeseburger "the Cadillac of burgers," and you can still get that burger if you order the Cadillac.

All of which is somewhat remarkable for a place that operates under the auspices of something called The Clarkes' Group LLC. But it's not any

Vintage Spot: Yorkville

ORWASHERS: EST. 1916

Though it now calls itself an "artisan bakery"—and its owner a "bread architect"—Orwashers still makes the loaves of its founder, Abraham Orwasher. In other words, you can still get the rye and pumpernickel, but now you can also get the Rustica Sesamo and Chardonnay Miche.

308 E. 78th St.; (212) 288-6569; orwashers.com

more remarkable than the survival of the place for the century or so before The Clarkes' Group LLC moved in.

The brick box appeared in 1868 and housed a bar in 1884. It wasn't Clarke's bar. It was first Jennings's bar and then Duneen's bar. Around 1902 Duneen hired a bartender named Patrick Joseph Clarke; in 1912 Duneen sold the bar, and it became P.J. Clarke's.

Paddy Clarke reputedly steered the place steadily through Prohibition, and later through the challenging changes in his surroundings. He died in 1948, and his family sold the bar to the Lavezzos, who owned the building, and also sold and restored antiques.

No doubt guided by their love of antiquity, the Lavezzos held on to the building. In 1967 they scored a ninety-nine-year lease. The little place laid low, while around it the buildings grew high. That's why P.J. Clarke's today looks like the neighboring building's doorstep.

Meanwhile, the stories piled up and somehow got preserved. They touch on subjects from a stuffed dog to Liza Minnelli. One story has it that Ernest Borgnine and Ethel Merman were at the bar when they announced their marriage, which famously ended in little more time than it took to announce.

Mercer supposedly wrote his song at the bar, on a bar napkin. Charles R. Jackson wrote *The Lost Weekend* at the bar, though probably on regular paper. Sinatra came in starting in the forties and insisted on table 20, which is still designated his table. With Frank, you never know.

In 2002 the bar was bought by investors including the restaurateur Phil Scotti, the Yankees owner George Steinbrenner, and the actor Timothy Hutton. They took on that ominous "LLC" name. They made longtime P.J. Clarke's regulars very afraid.

They closed the bar down and worked on it for more than a year. But in the end they seemed to have put everything back where it belonged. You know that there's been restraint when you can still open a door and glimpse men confronting five-foot-high, century-old urinals.

"We wanted to keep things as authentic as can be," says Nick Morand, the general manager of P.J. Clarke's. "Everything we've done here we tried to keep close to the original. It's a place to show off. It's something to be very proud of."

They were proud enough to put up two more Clarkes in Manhattan, and a Clarke each in Las Vegas, D.C., and São Paulo. But those are different sorts of Clarkes. No new place can be an old place. That's why the Group took care to let the old place keep all its allusions.

Downstairs, anyway. Upstairs, they got tougher. They remade the Lavezzos' apartment into a restaurant called Sidecar. It's sort of a Clarke's for grown-ups. It has its original brick walls, but beyond that, it's more refined. It has no urinals the size of bathtubs.

That's business, at least when you're an LLC. The new Sidecar undoubtedly helps the old Clarke's to go on. And it's still in the little old building, of which the Group is supremely proud, Nick says: "We caused Manhattan to build itself up around us."

PAPAYA KING

179 E. 86TH ST. • NEW YORK, NY 10028

(212) 369-0648 • PAPAYAKING.COM

Hot Dogs Meet the Tropics

Get your vitamins and antioxidants! Get the most powerful digestive known! Improve heart health! Control aging! All at a hot-dog stand!

It's a dream come true. Even more so if you believe it. And it makes the hot dogs taste even better, if that is possible. Good health from a hot-dog stand is as New York as papaya from a hot-dog stand, which is why they've both endured for eighty years at their original location.

The stand is Papaya King, except that its sign doesn't say "Papaya King." It says, DRINK VITAMIN PACKED HEALTH GIVING PAPAYA THE KING OF ALL DRINKS. If there were enough room, it might also say, "And since you have such a healthy drink, a couple of little frankfurters really couldn't hurt."

But it doesn't have to. You've already said it to yourself. A Papaya King hot dog is one of the most seductive things in Manhattan. The pungent stand is a daily party at which seemingly everyone in New York gets in line to pair the city's signature food with the tropics' signature nectars.

The food is a sausagian masterpiece of seasoning, suppleness, and snap, on a bun that is somehow at once perfectly soft and crunchy. The drinks are purees of, among other things, papaya, mango, and coconut, blended with flavors that put them in harmony with the masterpiece sausage.

The combination is not just uncommonly tasty but also uncommonly thrifty. Despite its regal authority, Papaya King does not lash you. A dog here is half the price of one at your favorite old New York delicatessen, and a quarter the price of one at your favorite new New York baseball stadium.

Plus, if you dine in, the stand provides entertainment that you just won't find at places with exorbitant hot dogs. You can look at the people serving the food. You can look at the people buying the food. And most of all, you can look at compelling facts celebrating the food.

Take your container. If you get a sixteen-ounce papaya, you'll have a cup that says: "Papayas contain three powerful antioxidants that control premature aging." Read on, and you'll also be delighted to learn things like: "Papayas promote heart health and male fertility."

Then take the walls. Also the windows, the drink tanks, and the counters. They offer more facts, by way of the store's little yellow signs. Many of the signs tell you more things you want to believe; a few tell you some things you might have preferred not to know.

From the first category: "'Papaya is the most powerful digestive known.'—Dr. Harvey Kellogg of the famous Battle Creek Sanitorium in Battle Creek, Michigan."

From the second: "Yankee slugger Babe Ruth once ate 12 hot dogs between games of a double header."

Dr. John Harvey Kellogg has been dead for seventy years, and the Babe has been gone for almost as long. But they belong here because they had colorful lives, and Papaya King's life has been colorful enough to encompass everything from hula girls to the Brooklyn Dodgers.

According to flexible legend, Gus Poulos, a Greek immigrant and deli owner, was on vacation in Miami (or Cuba) when he encountered the papaya. In that fruit he saw his future, since he had imagination, and since at the time papayas couldn't be found at your neighborhood grocery.

In 1932, at what's now Papaya King, he opened a stand he called Hawaiian Tropical Drinks, even though the fruit came from Florida. It had a bamboo sign, a palm-frond counter, suspended nets of pineapples, bananas, and coconuts, and at least one counter man wearing a pith helmet.

The drinks didn't sell. So Gus hired girls to wear hula skirts, stand on the corner, and hand out free drinks (or papaya chunks). Then the drinks sold.

Then Gus started opening stores in other locations, including Brooklyn, Baltimore, Philadelphia, and, curiously, Miami.

Still, his customers were hungry. And since his flagship was in an area called Germantown—and he had a German girlfriend—he decided to address their hunger with frankfurters. From this decision came not only one of the city's best culinary matings, but also the city's best hot-dog slogan: "Tastier Than Filet Mignon."

Years later—still in legend—a Brooklyn Dodger referred to Gus as the Papaya King, which was catchier than the Hawaiian Tropical Drinks King. Gus adopted the name for his store, and it proved catchy indeed: Lots of other guys proceeded to adopt versions of it for their stores.

Through the decades the city has hosted, among other places, Papaya Kingdom, Papaya Prince, Papaya Paradise, Papaya World, and Papaya Plus, not to mention Frank's Papaya, Mike's Papaya, Gray's Papaya, Original Papaya, just plain Papaya, and Papaya Dog.

Most are gone, though not Gray's, which was launched by a Papaya King worker, and which has become a landmark of its own, in two locations. There have also been other Papaya Kings, but, as with Hawaiian Tropical Drinks, lasting success came only to the original.

The original was passed down to Peter Poulos and Alexander Poulos, the son and nephew of Gus, who died in 1988. In 2010 the store was bought by a group of investors led by Wayne Rosenbaum, who had always loved it and who now lovingly runs it.

Wayne cleaned it and restored it, but he didn't defile it. The place is a bit shinier, yet it looks pretty much the same. It has its grand neon signs from the sixties, its grand steel tanks from the thirties, and most important, its grand hot dogs from a factory four miles away.

Wayne vows that he didn't get into it just for the free hot dogs. He also vows that he didn't get into it just for the money.

"We didn't buy a hot-dog stand," he says. "We bought seventy-eight years of history, New York City history. We bought people's memories."

POSEIDON GREEK BAKERY

629 NINTH AVE. • NEW YORK, NY 10036

(212) 757-6173

A Family Recipe

*Y*ou might start out caring about finikia and saragli, but you're bound to end up caring about Papou and Yiayia. That's because if it hadn't been for Papou and Yiayia, there almost surely wouldn't be any finikia and saragli.

Finikia are honey cookies and saragli are rolled baklava, and they look so good that you're amazed when they taste better than they look. That's when you start caring about Papou and Yiayia, because they're the grandpa and grandma responsible for the survival of Poseidon Greek Bakery.

You care about them, that is, if Lili Fable has told you about them, which she will if you ask and which she might if you don't. She is the daughter-in-law responsible for the survival of Poseidon, which she pronounces "Poe-see-don" and bills as THE GREAT GREEK BAKERY ON NINTH AVENUE.

Thanks to Papou, Yiayia, and Lili, among others, you can still walk into a shop and be dazzled by a profusion of traditional Greek pastries. And you can still walk into a shop that features not only Greek pastries but also a perfect depiction of 1952.

The shop moved to its current location in Hell's Kitchen that year and has barely changed in all the decades since. It's a little old bakery, from its original white-and-blue wooden counter fronts to the dozens of framed family photos crammed onto the shelves behind it.

But it's the glass cases you focus on, because they hold not only the finikia and the saragli, but also the kourambiedes and the koulourakia—the butter cookies and the egg biscuits. Also the trigona, the afali, and the kataif, plus several flavors of strudel, since Yiayia was actually Austrian.

Those are the sweets, but Poseidon also has the savories, including the tiropita, the kreatopita, and the spanakopita. They are, in order, the cheese pie, the meat pie, and the spinach pie. There's also Yiayia's vegetable pie, called Menina Mash, since Yiayia was actually Menina.

All of it is made from the original family recipes, and most of the pastry is made by Lili. If she's not at the counter, she's probably steps away in the kitchen at her marble slab, laying out phyllo squares, brushing them with soybean oil, spooning on their fillings, and folding them up like flags.

Speaking of America, Lili confidently claims that Poseidon is the only bakery in the country that still makes its own phyllo dough. And whenever she makes that claim, she follows it with a vow: "The day we buy phyllo in this store is the day I retire."

She's happy to talk to you about phyllo, even if it's to admonish you never to put it into a microwave oven. But she's happiest to talk to you about family, even if it's to tell you how her grandson Jordan learned to walk by hanging onto the tail of a golden retriever named Jake.

"He was the most patient dog," she says of Jake, and that quality seems to run in the family. It takes patience to spend hours a day on your feet folding pies. But Lili figures that she has yet to put in the patience that it took to keep the bakery on its feet in 1923.

It was in that year that the Greek immigrant Demetrios Anagnostou opened Poseidon on 41st Street between Eighth and Ninth Avenues. He named it for his bakery in Greece, which he had named for the god of the sea. His bakery was probably on the Ionian Sea. Here he settled for the Hudson River.

Papou, who was actually Michael, was his son. He eventually took over the bakery, then met Menina. She was an Italian-Austrian widow with three children. She was not Greek. But Michael saw in her a great wife, with a bonus of strudel recipes.

Vintage Spot: Hell's Kitchen

RUDY'S BAR AND GRILL: EST. 1934

The banquettes are upholstered almost entirely in red duct tape, which helps to explain why the beer is cheap and the hot dogs are free. This is the bar that defines "dive." Come early to squeeze in. Look for the six-foot pig and the wooden door whose windows spell out RUDY.

627 Ninth Ave.; (646) 707-0890; rudysbarnyc.com

In 1952 the Port Authority of New York & New Jersey informed the couple that they were in the way of a new ramp. They searched the neighborhood, found a deal, and bought the current building, which became the family's home and secured the bakery's future.

When Papou retired, Menina's sons, Anthony and John Fable, took over. When John retired, Anthony and his wife, Lili, took over. After fifty-two years between the two locations, Anthony retired. Lili and their son Paul took over. Paul, among other things, bakes cookies.

The Fables still live in the building, so the bakery's still part of their home, which explains why the bakery feels like part of a home.

It feels like part of a Greek home. But as Lili candidly points out, it isn't: "With Papou not here, there's not a single Greek in the store."

ROLF'S GERMAN RESTAURANT

281 THIRD AVE. • NEW YORK, NY 10010

(212) 477-4750 • ROLFSNYC.COM

Hot When It's Cold

Everyone knows the spots to see holiday spectacles in Manhattan. Not everyone knows that each could be topped by Rolf's German Restaurant. At Rockefeller Center, for instance, you can hang around a big tree. At Rolf's, by stunning contrast, you can hang around *in* a big tree.

"We try to present it as an old-fashioned, Victorian-style Christmas," says Bob Maisano, the owner of Rolf's and the spectacle director. "That seems to be the thing that people reflect about. We try to have it give you the feeling of sitting in or under a Christmas tree."

They succeed. From November through January, their interior is not just decked with, but nearly obliterated by, a profusion of mostly German Christmas antiques. It's a forest of glistening icicles, gleaming ball ornaments, and glowing lights. It's not a restaurant with decorations. It's decorations with a restaurant.

You sit, if you can find the seats, among pine branches laden with objects, accented by kaleidoscopic hand-blown Egyptian crystals. When you focus, the objects become, say, dolls with parasols, angels with fiddles, or three Santa Clauses enjoying a spot of Merlot.

The Santas may be there to remind you that you, too, can have refreshments, which would give you the time you need to process what you have seen. Rolf's is among the last of the old German restaurants in the city, and November through January is when the appeal of its kind of cuisine peaks.

The menu includes wiener schnitzel, rahm schnitzel, jaeger schnitzel, and schnitzel a la Holstein, along with weisswurst, knackwurst, bratwurst, smoked bratwurst, and the four-wurst platter. There's sauerbraten and sauerkraut and potato pancakes and spaetzle. And that's why if you don't like crowds, you visit Rolf's from June through August.

In summer, fake oak leaves replace the fake pine branches—but patrons, Bob says, replace Rolf's with outdoor cafes. "When people think of German, they think of Bavarian, which is what we are," he says. Not even the Egyptian crystals would do much to help.

Bob appreciates the summer break, as long as it's a break. But he says that it would never end if it weren't for the winter. "This pays for the whole year," he says. "In business you have to have some kind of gimmick. If we didn't have this Christmas here, we wouldn't have this business here."

No one imagined this Christmas when Rolf's began, of course. Still, Bob says, there were those who were sure that the restaurant would fail.

Rolf Hoffman came to New York from Munich in the sixties. He worked at a restaurant in the neighborhood then known as Germantown. But he chose to start his own place in a former German neighborhood. People laughed, unaware that Germantown would soon be a former German neighborhood, too.

Hoffman opened Rolf's in 1968 with all the requisite touches, from glowering waitresses in dirndls to oompah bands. He died in 1981. Ben House, who had been his chef, took over the restaurant and invited his friend Bob to help him run it.

It was Ben who decided that the restaurant needed more Christmas flair. He gave it a whole lot more Christmas flair, Bob says. "He filled it with those cheap silver garlands. Bells, too. There were three Christmas trees. And there were animated polar bears holding martini glasses."

He kept filling the place until there was no space left to fill: "You wouldn't know if it was a restaurant or a store that sold Christmas decorations. He loved Christmas decorations. He was born in December. He loved Christmas. It seemed like the business was secondary to that."

Ben died in 1996—two days after Christmas. Bob recalls his saying: "If only I could just make Christmas." Bob took over the restaurant, which meant he took over the decorating. But as a former designer, he had his own concept of decorations.

He retired the silver garlands and the pickled polar bears and started replacing them with the nineteenth-century German antiques. People started coming each year to watch the collection grow. Last year, he says, he had eighty-five thousand lights. He hasn't counted the rest.

The dirndls and the oompah bands are long gone, Bob says: "It's not all that necessary. Unless you're at Disney World." But he adds more leaves for Oktoberfest (which is in September), and he keeps adding to the three-month show that has made Rolf's what it is today.

He searches New England antique shops for new old things. He surveys the collection and gets rid of old old things. "Every year I look to see where I could have improved, and I write notes," he says. It takes six weeks, every day after closing, to get all the baubles up.

Newcomers, Bob says, "are just pretty much awestruck." Apparently, some of them are overcome. "Last year I caught a girl—she came prepared—with a shopping bag, climbing up to the ceiling. She brought scissors, or wire cutters, and she started cutting down decorations."

Most visitors are content to enjoy them. "What gives me the most pleasure is when people walk in the door and they're overwhelmed," Bob says. "Maybe they had a bad time somewhere. Maybe they had a bad day at work. And at least they walked in here and had a moment of happiness."

SAMMY'S ROUMANIAN STEAK HOUSE

157 CHRYSTIE ST. • NEW YORK, NY 10002

(212) 673-0330

Your Big Fat Jewish Dinner

*I*f you don't get invited to a lot of catered affairs, the best place in New York to get over it is Sammy's. It's a nightly spree of singing, dancing, drinking, wisecracking, and gluttony, and you're welcome if you're up for old songs, old jokes, and broiled meat.

Sammy's is the last survivor of the city's Romanian steak houses, and as it survived it evolved into something that the others never were. It fused Jewish-style cuisine with party-style entertainment in a suburban-style basement. Then it threw in cold vodka.

People compare it to a bar mitzvah, which isn't strictly accurate, since the majority of patrons tend to be well over thirteen. A wedding is closer. In any case, you get the meal, the booze, the music, and the chance to hold hands with strangers and run around tables doing the hora.

"It starts as a restaurant, then goes into a pub, then goes into a night-club, and it ends as the only Jewish disco in town," says Dani Luv, the lead entertainer. Older patrons tend to come early, he says. "They think, 'I have to have time to go to the hospital.' Old people are afraid to go to midnight with this dreck."

By "dreck" he means the delicacies of which you must partake if you really want to get into the spirit of things. They include chopped liver with gribenes (fried chicken skin) and schmaltz (rendered chicken fat), Roma-nian tenderloin steak, latkes (potato pancakes), and a chocolate egg cream. It's hard-core dreck.

The menu has a couple of broiled fishes and a couple of green salads, but Sammy's is not in business to help you maintain your sensible diet. You're here for debauchery. It's one night. As Dani announces from his keyboard when he starts his show: "Welcome to the House of Cholesterol."

You get a preview of your night in the house as soon as you arrive, in the hundreds of snapshots plastered on the walls, inside and out. They show patrons waving, kissing, hugging, groping, and always smiling. Look close for past merrymakers like Billy Crystal and Dick Clark.

Sit down at a table with a white tablecloth and white cloth napkins, which let you know that you are respected, even if you are in a basement. You'll see a glass pitcher of the type that elsewhere might hold pancake syrup but that here holds pure chicken fat. You get used to its shade of yellow.

Order the liver, and a seasoned waiter will appear with a shiny steel bowl and, with due flourish, toss in julienned white radish, fried onion, gribenes, and liver. He'll then grab your fat dispenser and pour the schmaltz in from on high, add salt and pepper, and mix. It's tangy. It's rich.

Around this time (for the liver's your appetizer), Dani will take his place at the keyboard, which is in the back corner directly in front of the loos. He is Israeli. He says he's known as the Israeli Frank Sinatra. And the Israeli Louis Armstrong. And the Israeli Robin Williams.

As you dine on a steak that's too long to fit on your plate—along with latkes—he'll sing numbers like "All of Me" and "Fly Me to the Moon." Also numbers like "It Had to Be Jew" and "The Girl from Emphysema."

He taunts the crowd ("You're not Jewish? No one is perfect"). And on occasion, so do the waiters. If they don't like your tie, they may cut it off—with your permission, of course, which they know you're more likely to grant when you've been mellowed by some Ketel One.

Before long, as predicted, you're bound to be up and romping, at first perhaps with one partner but eventually with many. The inducement builds as the music shifts to the Jewish and Israeli classics that get celebrants popping out of their chairs and running around in circles.

Finally, your table will be supplied with the ingredients for a classic egg cream: milk, seltzer in siphon bottles, and Fox's U-bet chocolate syrup. You can make your own, but support is available from the waiters. Milk with meat, of course, isn't kosher, but Sammy's is in no sense orthodox.

The precise origin of all this mirth is lost in time, but Romanian steak houses followed the arrival of Eastern European Jews in New York. There were several on the Lower East Side, where the immigrants generally settled. The places had chopped liver and tenderloin, though no electronic keyboards.

The origin of Sammy's itself came around 1927, says the restaurant's current owner, Dave Zimmerman. It either began as or eventually became the Parkway steak house, which was at the same address, on the second floor.

When the Parkway moved out in the fifties, Sammy Friedman moved in, and justifiably renamed it Sammy's Roumanian (with a U). He ran it till 1975, when Dave's father, Stan Zimmerman, won it from Sammy in a poker game.

Dave credits his father with turning Sammy's Roumanian into the perpetual reception it is today. Stan, he says, launched the tableside chopped-liver mixing, the do-it-yourself egg creams, the snapshot walls, the icy vodka, and most of all, the Catskills entertainment.

Sammy had had pianists, but Stan wanted showmen. He hired Tuvia Zimber, a wisecracking keyboardist, then Ruby Levine, a wisecracking violinist. He also hired Rob Taube, a Catholic keyboardist who somehow made a great Jew. Rob and Tuvia still appear.

Dave took over in 1996. He redid the kitchen and restrooms, for which he got no argument. And he relieved the menu of some ancient items that had a fast-shrinking fan base, including pitcha (calf's-foot jelly) and sliced brains (what it says).

He sums up the streamlined Sammy's: "Latke, vodka, chopped liver, steak." And he pridefully shares his most cherished review.

"My father gave me one compliment in my life," he says. "He said, 'I made my generation happy. But you make every generation happy.'"

SARDI'S

234 W. 44TH ST. • NEW YORK, NY 10036

(212) 221-8440 • SARDIS.COM

The Best Place to Hang

*Y*ou know you're a star in New York City when you get your face sketched by a currency engraver in Fort Worth. Which confirms that technology makes anything possible, and that there's still nothing quite like being hung up at Sardi's.

Sardi's is the restaurant that doubles as a gallery of caricatures of nearly a century's worth of celebrities. More than any other restaurant in the city, it revels in stardom. It's like the Hollywood Walk of Fame, except with pictures and no gum wads.

It's where you dine among a kaleidoscope of hundreds of famous faces from Lucille Ball to Walter Cronkite to Gene Kelly to Gore Vidal—many sporting pop-eyes, flap ears, jut chins, gap teeth, fright hair, glacier brows, pumpkin grins, pencil necks, and chipmunk cheeks.

In a culture that thrives on the transitory, Sardi's prizes permanence. Its stars stay stars not only after they're stars but also after they're dead. Naturally, this has irresistible appeal to people in show business. That's why they covet a call from Richard Baratz, the Fort Worth engraver.

Richard is the latest and longest-running of the Sardi's artists. He's been sketching the stars since 1974. He makes money, but not just at Sardi's. He works for the US Department of the Treasury, at the Bureau of Engraving and Printing, which some years ago sent him to Texas.

So now he sees his subjects in e-mails instead of in chairs, which apparently matters not at all to the subjects. They are forgiving of Richard's move, as he is forgiving of their features. Of all the Sardi's caricaturists, Richard has been the kindest.

"When I started, I was doing people like Myrna Loy and Katharine Hepburn," he says. "What am I gonna do, insult an elderly former star, a grand lady? They don't want to be insulted. So I always thought: Instead of insulting them, why not compliment them?"

He knows that such a thought is what turns caricatures into portraits. But the subjects have to sign the drawings, and not all will sign off on flap ears. The first artist managed to get the signature before he finished the drawing. "Then he went back to the house," Richard says, "and went to town with it."

That was Alex Gard, whose work rarely paid anyone compliments. But it still hangs, along with that of his successors. The drawings tell the story of American popular culture, which dovetails with the story of an unplanned showbiz hall of fame.

Clearly bound for theatrical lives, Melchiorre Pio Vincenzo Sardi and Eugenia Pallera met while working at a theatrical boarding house. Vincent got Jenny to marry him, though on the second try. He then continued to be a waiter, which is much like being an actor.

In 1921 the Sardis opened the Little Restaurant, so named because it was next door to the Little Theatre. Theater people found it, even though it actually was little, and they began the tradition of making the Sardis' place a second home. In 1927, with the help of the Shubert family, the Sardis opened Sardi's at the present location. It wasn't a hit. It needed something. And it got something, starting at a lunch meeting of a group of droll newsmen and press agents that called itself the Cheese Club.

One of the press guys brought along the unemployed Alex Gard. Gard drew caricatures of the attendant Cheeses. Vincent loved them. He hung them up. Then he remembered what had turned a Paris restaurant named Zelli's into a hit: caricatures.

Since Gard was starving and Sardi was struggling, they struck a symbiotic deal. Gard would give Sardi caricatures; Sardi would give Gard meals. It is said that Sardi agreed not to pan the drawings and that Gard agreed not to knock the cook.

Gard went on to give Sardi's around seven hundred caricatures, and Sardi's went on to give Gard around fourteen thousand meals. When Vincent Sardi Jr. took over after the Second World War, he offered Gard money. Gard stuck with the meals. This says something about Sardi's food.

The draw of the drawings, along with the charm of the Sardis, helped to make Sardi's the premiere Broadway haunt. It was home to deal-making, standing ovations, opening-night parties, a radio show, and the creation of the Tony Awards, which began at another lunch.

It was also a haven for actors dreaming of deals, ovations, and Tonys. Vincent Sr., who actually cared about them, established an Actors' Menu. To this day, a card-carrying thesp can avail himself of that menu and eat at a discount. No drawing is required.

Back at the drawing board, Alex Gard died in 1948. John Mackey came in for a couple of years, then Don Bevan came in for twenty. Bevan's caricatures were friendlier than Gard's, which made them more amusing. Bevan had a way of making chipmunk cheeks cute.

When Bevan left, Vincent Jr. held a contest to find his replacement. Richard won, with a caricature of Bette Midler (who despised it). He has since done around a thousand, at the rate of around thirty a year. Perhaps anticipating his job transfer, he didn't sign up for the meals.

Around the time that Richard came in, so did Max Klimavicius. By the time Vincent Jr. retired in the nineties, Max was in charge. Vincent Jr. had brought Max along, as Max has since been doing for Vincent Jr.'s grandson, Sean Ricketts.

"It started with the love of these two immigrants for the theater folk," Max says. "When Vincent Sardi Senior passed away, Vincent Sardi Junior found a chest of IOUs that had never been redeemed. He gave advice, he gave credit, and most of all he gave love."

SERENDIPITY 3

225 E. 60TH ST. • NEW YORK, NY 10022

(212) 838-3531 • SERENDIPITY3.COM

Expect the Unexpected

There's an advantage to choosing the Frrrozen Hot Chocolate over the Golden Opulence Sundae. That is, besides saving $991.05. True, you miss the experience of having a mouthful of gold. But you save enough to buy 111 more Frrrozen Hot Chocolates.

This sort of reasoning—and this sort of math—could only come up in one place: the one with a world-famous dessert for $8.95 and a world-record dessert for $1,000, not to mention a dessert made from a recipe on a can of condensed milk, for $7.50.

It's Serendipity 3, which got its name from a fairy tale, which is what it looks like, and more or less what it is. It's a dream come true for three dreamers who never exactly dreamed it. It's also a restaurant with dim sum, ravioli, bean burgers, and chicken potpie.

It's a little spot that's larger than life, a Munchkinland of mirrors, toys, fake potted cactus, and dozens of suspended stained-glass lampshades. It's a place to escape the normal world and to face abnormal choices, such as the one between a burger for $12.50 and one for $295.

You make your escape on a bentwood chair at an antique table, where you get a laminated calligraphed menu that's twenty inches tall. In there you'll find the above dishes, along with others including the caviar and sour cream omelet, the chili with cheese crepe, and the sautéed chicken livers.

Just remember that Serendipity 3 is renowned for its desserts, which include Karo pecan pie, Aunt Buba's Sand Tarts, and three-scoop sundaes—along with the Frrrozen Hot Chocolate, which also comes in a peanut-butter version and is listed as a drink just to throw you off.

It is not a drink. At least not in the conventional sense. If you try to consume it through a straw, you may harm yourself. It's a bowl of thick, creamy, crunchy, impossibly chocolatey chilly chocolate, topped with whipped cream, topped with chocolate. It probably can't be topped.

It really is world-famous and has been almost since it was invented, which was more than half a century ago. Its inventor was the dreamer who also dreamed up the restaurant's name, which has proved prophetic, since Serendipity 3 has been truly serendipitous.

It began with the convergence of three aspiring actors and dancers named Stephen Bruce, Patch Carradine, and Calvin Holt. In the fifties they became roommates in a fourth-floor walkup in the West 20s, where their destiny was determined by talents other than dancing.

Patch and Calvin had a feel for food, Stephen says. "They were both from the South, and had recipes from aunts, uncles, and grandparents. They automatically knew how to give a party." Stephen automatically knew how to find stuff and arrange it.

So they gave parties, and the guests complimented the refreshments and the decor. Some of them wanted the recipes. Some of them wanted the furniture. The men decided to open a place that sold food and artifacts, to help pay for the dancing lessons they were still determined to take.

They opened it in 1954, in a basement on East 58th Street. Patch named it with a word Horace Walpole coined in reference to a Persian fairy tale called "The Three Princes of Serendip." The menu included espresso from a twenties espresso maker, and Lemon Icebox Pie from the condensed-milk can.

Mindful of their budget, Stephen decorated in all white, except for colorful Tiffany-style lampshades, which back then came cheap. Everything worked. "To my surprise we were an immediate success," Stephen says. "In the first ten days, we had lines out the door."

Vintage Spots: Upper East Side

BEMELMANS BAR AT THE CARLYLE: EST. 1947

It got its name after Ludwig Bemelmans ringed it with murals of whimsical Central Park scenes, including his *Madeline* characters. It has pianists and jazz trios, which can be supplemented with the likes of twenty-one-dollar cocktails and twenty-five-dollar hamburgers.

35 E. 76th St.; (212) 744-1600; rosewoodhotels.com

DONOHUE'S STEAK HOUSE: EST. 1950

The dining room with the wood paneling and the black tufted booths make this look like it should be Donohue's Coffee Shop. Either way, it's a little hideaway, favored by older patrons, who are content to dine in peace amid old sea paintings and glowing sconces.

845 Lexington Ave.; (212) 744-0938

JIM'S SHOE REPAIRING: EST. 1932

Across from the six high shoeshine chairs are six low waiting chairs—in individual wooden booths with footstools and little doors. While you wait, you can read about the shop in clips on the wall, like a 1949 "Little Old New York" column written by Ed Sullivan.

50 E. 59th St.; (212) 355-8259; jimsshoerepair.com

LE VEAU D'OR: EST. 1937

Come here for a cozy meal of canard rôti aux cerises (roast duck with cherry sauce) or tripes à la mode de Caen (tripes with Calvados). Once a refuge for people like Orson Welles and Grace Kelly, it's now a refuge for people who remember Orson Welles and Grace Kelly.

129 E. 60th St.; (212) 838-8133

The lines grew when Patch got creative with an appliance that he favored for his own libations. "He decided to use a blender to mix thirteen kinds of chocolate with milk and ice," Stephen says. "It became so famous so quickly because, at the time, no one else had decided to do dessert in a blender."

They had too much success for a basement, so within a few years they moved Serendipity 3 to its current home on East 60th Street. They added fashions designed by Stephen to the food and artifacts—and they lured stars. Among them, Stephen says, was Marilyn Monroe.

"One day she called me and said, 'Steve, I'm so glad you're there. I have a movie opening to go to and I can't decide what to wear.' She was a size 8. I had a size 6. She said, 'That's perfect. It'll fit me better that way.' So at nine o'clock at night we went into the ladies' room and I stuffed her into it and sewed up the back."

Stephen, the sole owner since Patch and Calvin died, has clearly determined to keep Serendipity 3 full of surprises. That's why, for its fiftieth birthday, he unveiled the Golden Opulence Sundae, featuring Tahitian vanilla ice cream wrapped in gold leaf—for a cool thousand.

He followed that up with Le Burger Extravagant, comprising (in part) Wagyu beef, black truffles, and a fried quail egg on a gold-flecked roll topped with caviar ($295).

After all, surprises attract surprises. But Stephen may never get another one like the one he remembers best.

"One day there was a knock on the door at ten in the morning," he recalls. "I opened the door, and a woman said, 'How much is that candlestick in zee window?' I recognized Garbo. She came in, and we talked about the candlestick. She was a recluse, but we had a conversation for ten to twelve minutes.

"Then a waiter carrying a stack of ten plates looks over and sees her. He yells, 'Oh my God, it's Garbo! And he drops the dishes on the tile floor. She runs out the door and never comes back. But to this day I treasure my moments with her."

THE SILVERSMITH

184¾ W. FOURTH ST. • NEW YORK, NY 10014

(212) 924-5266

Just Try to Fit In

You don't touch Honey below the neck, and you don't touch Spartacus anywhere. These are the rules, and they get to make them. They live here. And they're big.

Honey and Spartacus are alley cats, which is fitting, since they live in an alley. More precisely, they live in a shop that was built into an alley. They are the rulers of The Silversmith, a jewelry store that, with more than four people and two cats inside, wouldn't have room for the jewelry.

They are assisted by Ruth Kuzub, who slightly predates them. She has been working in the store since 1960. Thus, for over half a century, she's been making jewelry, selling jewelry, and fixing jewelry. And feeding cats. In a room that's seven steps long.

The Silversmith is indeed wedged between two buildings, which is why its street number is 184¾. According to Ruth, the store was built in 1938 for a coppersmith. It's among the city stores crammed into alleys to keep the rent affordable for cats.

Throughout its seven steps you are flanked by weathered wooden wall cases displaying the necklaces, bracelets, earrings, bands, and brooches. Outside the door are tables and racks displaying more jewelry. Without the outdoor displays, most people would probably miss the indoor displays.

Back inside, the floor space is approximately one person wide and indeed allows you about seven steps to the sales counter. Behind the counter is Ruth's desk, with its drawer stuffed with jewelry tools. In front of the counter is Honey's bed. The cats hid the litter box.

Ruth once made all the jewelry, since she's a genuine Village artist, but at a moment she prefers to forget, she fell and broke her wrists. She had to start buying jewelry. "Things would fall out of my hand," she says. "I was afraid to hold the torch for fear it would fall."

She still displays some of her work, but she supplements it with pieces from sources including Ireland, Israel, Poland, and Indonesia. She has amber from the Baltic Sea and turquoise from American Indians. Also bracelets from California and silver from New Jersey.

Now in her eighties, she opens the store just in the evenings. If she has to leave for a while, she puts up a sign and leaves. She closes the store but leaves the outside part of it open, since that is always manned by personnel other than cats.

Either way, the store has a steady flow of visitors, including neighbors who come by just to say hello to Ruth. In many ways, more than any other place, The Silversmith takes you back to the Greenwich Village we like to think Greenwich Village still is, even though it isn't.

Ruth came to that Village from Cleveland, ready to sing and dance, since that's what she had been doing in Cleveland. She sang and danced for a while, notably in the mid-fifties in the Broadway production of the musical *Fanny,* and as a Copa Girl.

Around that time, two women named Jen Young and Cicely Nemis opened a silver workshop in a basement on Jones Street. They called it The Silversmith. In 1958 they added the current location as a jewelry shop. Back then, Ruth says, the place was even smaller.

The alley shop, she says, was built by a landlady named Mrs. Shapiro for the late Spanish copper artist Francisco Rebajes. "Mrs. Shapiro wanted to have a store for artists," she says. "Rebajes made copper jewelry." He also lived in the store with his wife.

Other artists moved in after Rebajes moved out. And Ruth came to The Silversmith after Jen moved out. She took a job with Cicely, because she loved the neighborhood scene. "The Village was full of artists," she says. "The streets were full of artists."

She began in 1960 and spent six months working the counter. "I said, 'God, it's boring sitting here doing this. Give me something to do.' She said, 'OK. Here. Saw this.' So I sawed it. And that's how I became a jeweler."

By 1969 Cicely was gone and Ruth was running the store. She has always run it with cats, though she once she ran it with cats and a dog. You make room. Or you try. "I would love to have a bigger store," she says. "I don't have room for display."

There are other disadvantages: "I've been held up, I've been tied up, I've had a knife at my throat, I've had a gun in my face. The store has been burglarized four times." The cats have been of no help. Ruth has since augmented them with alarm systems and a security camera.

For the truth is, she mostly loves her little store. Except for the knives and guns, it makes her feel safe and secure. "It's very unique. It's very cozy. When you close the door it feels wonderful." She closes the door. It feels wonderful. "See?" she says. "It's very peaceful."

It stays that way, as long as you don't touch Honey below the neck or Spartacus anywhere. They're just not people cats. And Ruth will be even more peaceful, she says, once she gets back to making her jewelry. Even if there still is nowhere to put it.

"I made anything, everything," she says wistfully. "I prefer to do my own work, because I'm supposed to be an artist expressing myself. I'm the one who designs the shoes; I don't want to be the shoemaker. Put it that way."

STRAND BOOK STORE

828 BROADWAY • NEW YORK, NY 10003

(212) 473-1452 • STRANDBOOKS.COM

Keeping You Curled Up

The Strand has not only outlived all of the bookstores of Book Row, it has also outlived Book Row. And it may end up outliving books.

In the past few years, it's become more organized, accessible, and comfortable. Needless to say, this has agitated some of its customers. But while it may have gotten refined, it's still one of the world's great bookstores, and still New York City's greatest literary treasure hunt.

The Strand is what lovers of books might drift through in their dreams: a Shangri-La of shelves, with a million new, old, and rare books. It's a New York Public Library where your books are never due. And though you have to pay for them, most are sold at a discount.

It's three floors and a basement, not to mention twenty-eight sidewalk carts, with stuff you'll never find at a regular bookstore, assuming you can find one. You'll entertain thoughts that the Strand has every book ever made. It doesn't. But over time, it might. It buys thousands of books every day.

You can head straight for a single category or wander through the stacks and get humbled by the profusion of works you know you'll never read. Some are literally out of reach, except to eight-foot patrons. But ladders are available, allowing you to climb to forbidden fruit.

Among the store's trademarks are the review copies of new books, which the Strand gets in large quantities and sells at half price. But most books are indeed marked down, and they're marked way down on the carts, where many books are a dollar and none is more than five.

Vintage Spot: Gramercy

MOLLY'S PUB and RESTAURANT: EST. 1964

When the real logs are burning in the real fireplace, this place is mighty cozy, if not mighty quiet. It claims roots in the 1890s, and it serves things like Irish lamb stew. It also keeps sawdust on the floor and calls itself a *shebeen,* which means, loosely, "naughty bar."

287 Third Ave.; (212) 889-3361; mollysshebeen.com

If you prefer your books marked up, just go up to the third floor. There you'll find the rare-book room, where the bargains are metaphysical. Recent choices have included *The World As I See It,* inscribed by Einstein, for $4,000, and James Joyce's *Ulysses,* illustrated by Henri Matisse and signed by Joyce and by Matisse, for $45,000.

For some customers, that's a steal. For other customers, that's a salary. The Strand is famous for being a bookstore for everyone. It has survived because of its prices, its location, its selection, and its adventure. But most of all, it has survived because of its family.

The family began with Benjamin Bass, a collector of books, who in 1927 opened a little bookstore on Eighth Street. He soon moved it to Fourth Avenue, known for decades as Book Row, which at its peak comprised approximately four dozen bookstores.

He probably named his store for *The Strand Magazine,* a British literary monthly (whose life closely paralleled that of Book Row). He may have named it for the London literary street, but since the magazine was named for the street, he essentially named it for both.

Benjamin's son Fred grew up in the store. At thirteen he was running errands; eventually he was running the store. He tried detours with jobs at places like Gimbels and Joey Gold's Theatre Ticket Service, but it was too late. The Strand already had him permanently booked.

In 1957 Benjamin and Fred moved the Strand to Broadway, and soon Fred was in charge, though Benjamin worked there till he died. Since then, Fred Bass has been the face of the Strand, when you can see his face. It's usually down, while he's appraising the latest load of incoming books.

In 1989 Fred was joined by his daughter, Nancy. A few years later, they opened a big new Strand on Fulton Street. They closed it a dozen years later, but not before it apparently inspired them to spruce up their flagship, which for all its charm was increasingly in need of sprucing.

By the nineties, the Strand harbored more than just worn floors, sprung shelves, and peeled pipes. It harbored human gridlock, which was robbing the hunt of its fun. People waited in line to get in, waited in line to get out, and waited in line to get around. The books were ousting the readers.

The Basses announced a renovation, the first in the store's history, promising petrified fans that the new store would definitely harbor no Starbucks. They spent a couple of million dollars and in 2003 unveiled a surprising hybrid of cluttered old shop and glossy new bookstore.

It has new wood floors that look like old wood floors, new bookshelves that look like old bookshelves, and red spray-painted signs that look like the old signs because they are. It has new bathrooms, a new elevator, its first new coat of paint, and a new invention called air-conditioning, which Fred tolerates.

In today's Strand, you'll find Sushi Sticky Notes, Mustache Push Pins, Oinking Bag Clips, and e-reader sleeves, though one is covered with pictures of old telephones. You'll find a candy store at the checkout and weekly events in the rare-book room. You'll find The Great Writers Finger Puppets. (They're Tolstoy, Shakespeare, Woolf, and Dickens.)

Vintage Spot: Union Square

PETE'S TAVERN: EST. 1864

Its claim to immortality is posted on the wall: "In this booth O. Henry wrote 'Gift of the Magi' in the year 1905." Above the booth is a TV screen. Pete's blends the old and the new. This is further evident in the meticulous labeling of the framed eight-by-tens of even more recent celebrities.

129 E. 18th St.; (212) 473-7676; petestavern.com

But crowd pleasers are a budget price for sustaining a colossal bookstore, not to mention two colossal book warehouses, in the digital age. Fred is ever practical: "Essentially," he says, "what we're trying to do is what our customers are asking for."

That philosophy has made the Strand not only a Book Row survivor but also one of the country's biggest used bookstores. For years its tagline was "8 Miles of Books." Now it's "18 Miles of Books." The mileage is an estimate, since Fred has no time to measure.

At roughly the age of his store, he still comes in every day and mostly does what he loves best, which is buying people's books. While his customers search for their treasures, he's at his counter searching for his. The only difference now is that, on warm days, he has to bundle up.

TOWN SHOP

2273 BROADWAY • NEW YORK, NY 10024

(212) 724-8160 • TOWNSHOP.COM

They Give You a Lift

*A*t the bra-fitting capital of New York, two things seem to be missing: the tape measures and the bras. But they only seem to be missing. The bras are in drawers accessible only to the staff, because if you were able to choose your own size, you wouldn't have to be here. And there never were any tape measures because, as you swiftly learn, "finding a perfect bra is an art, not a science."

The Town Shop has made that its motto; it has made "Your Support Is Our Business" its slogan. And it has proudly upheld both since before the brassiere had its patent. That's why, even today, steps away from a Victoria's Secret, it remains a destination for women convinced that it has the right foundations.

The shop may at first seem a lot like that upstart competitor: Its sales floor is fluffy with negligees, camisoles, bustiers, slips, and gowns. But you rarely make it to those before a fitter offers assistance while giving you the once-over, so she knows precisely how she can assist.

The shop's supposition, which has more or less turned into fact, is that 80 percent of women are running around in bras that don't fit. The shop's philosophy, as explained by the senior fitter, Eyvette Manigault, is that "a tape measure doesn't give you the right size for your bra. People think it does, but it doesn't. Every bra fits differently."

With the main tool of their trade banished, the fitters are left with nothing but the other main tool of their trade: their eyes. The Town Shop claims that every one of its dozen and a half fitters can, with a glance, discern the number and letter of a conventionally dressed woman.

Despite a considerable track record, some customers just don't believe it. They fight back. Eyvette confides that they're wasting everybody's time. A successful fitting in the dressing room, she says, takes fifteen to thirty minutes, "but if you get in there with them and they give you a hard time, it takes an hour."

Don't let this happen to you. Trust in the fitters' art. The Koch family does, which is why its business has spanned three centuries.

The shop is run by Danny Koch and his father, Peter Koch, the son of the late owner Selma Koch, the daughter-in-law of the founder, Samuel Koch. Samuel opened a notions shop on Bleecker Street in 1888, and eventually his three children were running shops of their own.

The stores had several names, but the one that prevailed was Town Shop, though no one seems to know where it came from. But a midcentury brochure promises that "Here you will find gay printed frocks to wear beneath smart ensemble coats, and adorable handmade undies to delight the most feminine person."

The other stores closed, but the Town Shop endured on the Upper West Side, and it became a favorite of big names who will understandably remain nameless. But the store won its greatest fame not for its star patrons, but for its star owner: Selma Koch.

Selma Lichtenstein married Samuel's son Henry Koch, learned bra-fitting from Henry's sister, and went to work for the family. She stayed on for seventy-five years, during which her skill, combined with her sass, made her a favorite of magazine, radio, and TV interviewers.

"She was tough," Danny says. "She was very tough. She had no problem whatsoever saying you are wrong. She loved saying that you are wrong even if you are partially right. . . . But if you keep on doing something that you love over and over again, and you demonstrate to people how much you love it, it becomes endearing."

She did what she loved long enough to fit the daughters of the daughters of the daughters of her original customers. "Sometimes a lady will come in with either a walker, or a wheelchair, or a nurse," she was quoted as saying in 2002. "She can barely move and she'll say to me, 'You know, you sold me my trousseau.'"

In those last years, Danny says, Selma herself came in with a walker. She wanted to die in the store, he adds, and she nearly made it. But she was in the hospital in 2003 when she was finally forced to quit her job, at the age of ninety-five. She earned a cheeky obituary in the *New York Times.* "When she died," Danny says, "it was as if a huge celebrity had died."

Since then, Danny and Peter have successfully carried on, partly by staying out of the way while the fitters do their work.

They order the biggest brand names in bradom, in numbers from 28 to 48 and in letters from AA to K. Few women are left out. Needless to say, the bras do not come at Target prices. But Target will let you out with the wrong brassiere. The Town Shop won't.

"If a woman has a pair of shoes that don't fit, she'll never wear it again," Danny says, "but a bra that doesn't fit correctly can be worn for fifteen years." Eyvette Manigault distills the fitting errors down to the most common: "Too small in the cup and too big around the rib cage."

Eyvette came to the store in 1971, and now it's she who pops up in the magazine stories and on the TV shows. The Koches like it that way; they seem intuitively to know that two guys are not the best possible media ambassadors for reputable bra-fitting.

Still, Danny loves the store, which surprises no one more than him. He's also an actor and, frankly, he never saw himself in ladies' underwear. "It's a very special business," he says. "I had no interest in being in it, and in a short time I understood the value of it."

Undoubtedly, so did Selma. She just chose other words to express it.

"What's the big deal?" she was quoted as saying, in her obit. "I'm just selling bras."

'21' CLUB

21 W. 52ND ST. • NEW YORK, NY 10019

(212) 582-7200 • 21CLUB.COM

Enjoy the Privileges

It's somehow fitting that the dominant feature of a New York City barroom known as a retreat for powerful men is a giant collection of toys. Of course, they're not just any toys. They are *the* Toys—a defensible title for toys that are in what's arguably *the* Barroom. It's not the barroom for everyone, and it's not everyone's barroom, but few such places in the world are as famous as '21.'

It's the haunt of presidents, movie stars, billionaires, and anyone else who's willing to dress like a grown-up and to part with thirty-two bucks for a burger. It's the place with the iron jockeys; with the five-thousand-pound door; with the wine cellar that still has a bottle of Sammy Davis Jr.'s wine.

It doesn't look so special. It looks like a barroom. That could be why its main dining room is, in fact, called the Bar Room. It has red-and-white-checked tablecloths, a bar with no stools, and The Toys. But you know that it's about more than burgers and chicken hash.

Indeed, since it's called a club, people think that they can't get in, says Avery McClanahan, the '21' marketing manager. "We've had people ask how to join; if there's a wait list; what the dues are," she says. "People ask, 'Am I allowed to drink at the bar?' Sometimes it's plain baffling."

The "club" name is compounded by the restaurant's mildly forbidding entrance, which features an iron fence and three dozen of those jockeys. "It confuses people sometimes. They wonder: Are we the Jockey Club? Are we a museum? Are we a funeral home?"

Granted, you don't see a lot of funeral homes with jockeys. But you don't see a lot of bars with them, either.

The first jockey arrived in the thirties, when a regular, possibly Alfred Vanderbilt, presented it in gratitude for the bar's hospitality. Horse people who frequented '21' liked the idea and sent their own jockeys. The jockeys decided to line themselves up in front of the building.

Meanwhile, a regular who ran British Airways had come in with a model plane and asked to hang it up above his table. "Nobody thought of the repercussions," Avery says. They comprised hundreds more promotional planes, trains, trucks, and boats, most of which got hung.

They were joined by mementos including a baseball bat from Willie Mays, a golf club from Jack Nicklaus, a tennis racket from John McEnroe, a pool cue from Jackie Gleason, a model PT-109 from John Kennedy, and a model Air Force One from Bill Clinton.

The Toys hide most of the Bar Room's ceiling. But they reveal only a bit of the bar's history.

Its history began when Jack Kriendler and his cousin Charlie Berns addressed Prohibition pragmatically by opening a speakeasy. They launched the Red Head, in Greenwich Village, in 1922. A few years later, they ditched the Red Head to open the fancier Fronton. Forced out by subway construction, they moved to the future site of Rockefeller Center and opened the Puncheon—which was forced out by Rockefeller Center. They bought the brownstone at 21 W. 52nd St., and on New Year's Eve 1929 patrons carted pieces of the Puncheon to the new Jack and Charlie's '21.'

Though the bar had a clubby look, it was never an actual club. Still, the clientele were, in a sense, club members. '21' was a place for everybody as long as he was somebody. Jack and Charlie were known for serving only the finest to only the finest.

But they were still running a speakeasy, which meant that it could be raided, which wouldn't do for a restaurant that's full of the finest. So they installed a raid-defense system highlighted by bottle-dumping bar shelves and a two-and-a-half-ton brick door cut into a basement wall.

That was the door to the wine cellar, rigged to be unlocked by the insertion of a skinny rod like a meat skewer into a hole. In 1932 agents scoured the place for hours and never found its two thousand cases of wine. Then again, they'd come without meat skewers.

Ironically, it was after repeal that the customers started to stray. Many left to try out the new clubs that were naturally popping up. Before long, though, '21' was not only winning back its old guests but also assembling one of the city's most formidable lists of new ones.

The Bar Room has stories to tell about Frank Sinatra, Katharine Hepburn, Ernest Hemingway, and Legs Diamond, the last two being in the same story. Other guests have included Groucho Marx, Grace Kelly, Alfred Hitchcock, and every president since Franklin Roosevelt, up to Bill Clinton.

Through the years, Kriendler and Berns added on two brownstones and several brothers, but by the eighties the last brother, Pete Kriendler, was done. The Kriendler and Berns families sold the restaurant to Marshall Cogan, reportedly for an appropriate $21 million.

The place got a makeover then and another one in the nineties, when it was sold to Orient-Express. In 2008 it stopped requiring men to wear ties. It's not the place it was in the old days. But no place from the old days is.

And there are a lot of things left from the old days, besides the jockeys and The Toys, which you can still see on a '21' tour. The most sobering of them is the brick door, behind which you can inspect the unused wine bottles of not only Sammy but also of James Stewart and Elizabeth Taylor.

"'21' is like being welcomed into a good friend's home," Avery says. "It's not Mom's home; you don't get to put your feet up on the furniture. But there is that comfort and that warmth. It's your club. It's everybody's club. And you don't have to pay dues."

VILLAGE VANGUARD

178 SEVENTH AVE. SOUTH • NEW YORK, NY 10014

(212) 255-4037 • VILLAGEVANGUARD.COM

A Celebrated Cellar

ot everyone who's been on the stage gets to be on the walls, but everyone who's gotten to be on the walls has been on the stage. That includes John Coltrane, Miles Davis, Dizzy Gillespie, Branford Marsalis, Charles Mingus, Thelonious Monk, and Stanley Turrentine. And not everyone who could be on the walls if he wanted to is on them; space is also taken up by the sousaphone and Jabbo Smith's double-bell euphonium.

They are the walls of the Village Vanguard, distinguished not only by their photographs (and brass) but by their support of one of the world's most fabled jazz clubs. And the Village Vanguard is distinguished not only by its walls, but by its survival within them for approximately eighty years.

It survived as a pre-Beat underground den for poetry readings, as a pre-Revival hootenanny for Lead Belly and Josh White, as a nightclub for acts from Lee Wiley to Professor Irwin Corey, and as an early stop for stars like Harry Belafonte and Barbra Streisand.

It survived for its first half century because of its founder, Max Gordon, who also ran one of the city's most glamorous clubs, the Blue Angel. And it's surviving in its second half century because of his widow, Lorraine Gordon, who had never run a club before but has been running one since he died.

"It's not something I ever thought I would do," says Lorraine, who is in her nineties. "I never thought he would die. I came in cold turkey. But I'm glad I did it, because it's been a very heartwarming experience." Partly for her, and possibly more for 123 people a night.

They climb down the stairs to the soothing room once known as the Golden Triangle, which somehow promises to give you a taste of a night in the old Village. It has a little bar at one end, a little stage at the other end, and little tables with chairs in the middle. Everything you need.

You get a laminated menu that offers drinks but no food, and that thanks you for "observing our QUIET policy during the music." It doesn't state the policy, but the gist of it is that if you create a disturbance during the show, Lorraine herself may come shut you up.

On a given night, you can quietly watch, say, the Fred Hersch Trio, the Bill Charlap Trio, or the Ravi Coltrane Quartet (starring John and Alice's son). And on a Monday night, you can watch the Village Vanguard Jazz Orchestra, since it has claimed most Monday nights since 1966.

It's a sixteen-piece band with the kind of sound that most Americans haven't heard since Johnny Carson left *The Tonight Show.* The sixteen pieces pack the stage. "If we were gonna do more," says John Mosca, the band's leader, "we'd have to start hiring smaller guys."

Max, he says, was eager to experiment with Monday nights. He liked new ideas. That's why it's called the Vanguard. He came to New York from Oregon apparently to make his contribution to art. He opened a tiny club called the Village Fair in 1932. He closed that and opened a club on Charles Street, then moved it to Seventh Avenue South. In 1935 it became the Village Vanguard.

It began with the poetry: "People threw money on the floor—that's how the poets got paid," Lorraine tells Barry Singer in her book *Alive at the Village Vanguard.* "It was kind of a coffee house without coffee, and no liquor license. I don't know what they drank. It was an intellectual gathering."

Later, Max brought in the folk singers, the comedians, and the pop singers. In 1943 he opened the Blue Angel on East 55th Street with Herbert Jacoby. He moved many Village Vanguard acts to the uptown club; among them were Pearl Bailey, Harry Belafonte, and Eartha Kitt.

Lorraine loved jazz even as a teenager in Newark, New Jersey. She had a thing for Benny Goodman—and went to jazz jams at the Village Vanguard. Auspiciously, she married the founder of the Blue Note jazz-record label, Alfred Lion. She helped Blue Note bloom, but the marriage eventually wilted.

She met Max on Fire Island and pitched him Thelonious Monk. Max booked Monk later that year at the Vanguard, and Monk tanked. But Max and Lorraine still married, and in 1957—whether or not through Lorraine's influence—the Village Vanguard became a jazz club.

Ironically, this time Lorraine stayed out of the business. She followed her own pursuits and left the two clubs to Max. But posh clubs were soon to be stranded for suburbia and television. The Blue Angel succumbed in 1964. It was the basement downtown that hung on.

The Vanguard went on to showcase the biggest names in jazz, and to turn some of smallest names in jazz into more of the biggest. Two of the big names formed the Thad Jones–Mel Lewis Orchestra, which was the start of the band that still plays every Monday night.

When Max died, Lorraine says in her book, she closed the club for the night. "And the next day I was there working, and it was open. And from that day on I've been there. In charge. Totally." She works in an office that was once the kitchen. She takes reservations.

The Gordons got some breaks—particularly the club's acoustics, which are undoubtedly as good as club acoustics get. Dozens of jazz albums have been recorded at the Vanguard, and at least for sound quality, there's not a bad seat in the house.

But Max and Lorraine's devotion is what has kept the place going, and made it a destination for the jazz fans of the world.

"Some nights no English is spoken here," Lorraine says. "It takes a long time to achieve that. You have to be doing something right, obviously."

WO HOP RESTAURANT

17 MOTT ST. • NEW YORK, NY 10013

(212) 267-2536 • WOHOPNYC.COM

The Other Great Walls

*J*f Wo Hop doesn't have the most authentic Chinese food, it at least has the most authentic inauthentic Chinese food. And since inauthentic Chinese food is authentic American food, Wo Hop does have the most authentic Chinese food. Or anyway, really good wontons.

Wo Hop may be New York City's most cherished restaurant for what most Americans grew up thinking was Chinese food—even though much of it was food invented for Americans by shrewd Cantonese cooks who no doubt foresaw the bonanza in takeout.

Wo Hop's been around since 1938, so it's nostalgic for most generations, which explains why so many members of them line up to get in. And they'll keep lining up as long as sources like *New York* magazine praise the food with terms like "soy sauce–soaked," "heavily battered," and "corn starch–thickened."

Here's where you come home to egg rolls, spare ribs, lo mein, chow mein, chow fon, egg foo young, and moo goo gai pan, not to mention crispy noodles, roast pork fried rice, hot tea, and fortune cookies ("Rice & Crisp Noodles Not Include with Orders").

And it is like coming home, since Wo Hop is in a basement, and except for the menus, it could just as well be your basement. It has tutti-frutti tables, green-and-white tile floors, old wooden chairs, and walls plastered with personal stuff, even if it isn't yours.

You are served by waiters in white shirts and blue linen jackets. The waiters are numbered; the food is not. There are no Columns A and B; there

Vintage Spot: Chinatown
CUP & SAUCER: EST. 1939

It has new red-white-and-blue menu boards, but that's somehow appropriate, since it's a good old red-white-and-blue luncheonette. And the updated boards are offset by the weathered Coca-Cola signs, the wood paneling, and the orange-topped stools on bases that look like bowling pins.

89 Canal St.; (212) 925-3298

are no combination platters. You get what you want, you get a lot of it, and you get most things for under twelve bucks.

While you're getting it, you can take a closer look at the personal stuff, and when you're done, you can make a personal contribution. At most restaurants you get to be on the wall only if you've become famous. At Wo Hop you get to be on the wall if you've got something to put on it.

The walls are especially popular with the potentially famous, who contribute headshots in hopes of realizing their potential. There are eight-by-tens bearing names like Rhett Kalman, Lindsay Esrig ("XOXO Lindsay"), and Randy Zanghi, who jauntily signed: "I'll have the eggplant parmigiana!!"

But there are also scores of snapshots, along with other territorial markers, including college and high-school IDs, business cards, and promotional stickers. One wall displays patches from our nation's finest and bravest, including the Coronado Police and the Roslyn Hills Fire Department.

You post your image at your own risk; when you return, you're likely to find that you've been enhanced with tattoos, freckles, stubble, unibrow, or dilated nostrils. But you'll probably still be there, which, besides the food, is what gets a lot of devotees to keep returning.

Steve Lippman frequented Wo Hop when he was in college. He moved to California more than thirty years ago. But you can still catch him here each year seated beside his younger self. "It's like a second home," he says. "This restaurant brings back the memories."

Past lives are indeed a draw, says Ming Huang, Wo Hop's manager. "People say, 'I was here when I was a teenager, and my picture is here.' They come from all over the country, especially in the summer. They try other kinds of Chinese food, and they don't like it."

Still, Wo Hop began as a Chinese restaurant for the Chinese. "At the time, there were not many Chinese here," Ming says. "Chinatown was very small. They only served limited Chinese food—wonton soup, congee, herbal tea—mostly to Chinese customers."

But by then, Chinatown was already an attraction, and it wasn't long before Wo Hop was catering to the crowds. "In 1938 our customers were eighty percent Chinese and twenty percent Americans," Ming says. "In 1980 they were ninety percent Americans and ten percent Chinese."

Wo Hop was founded by Bon Leung and Wah Lee, Ming says, and it's still owned by John Leung, Bon Leung's son. In 1976 a partner opened another Wo Hop upstairs. The menu is similar. But the place isn't. It's contemporary. It's sunny.

The original itself has been renovated, but it's hard to tell. It still looks like an old basement, because it still is. They just freshened the place a bit and added new tabletops. They took all the stuff off the walls, Ming says, and then they put it all back.

Because the legend has grown, and because there are only eleven tables, it can sometimes take half an hour to get in. But people don't seem to mind. They just stand on the steps and wait. Wo Hop means "peaceful together," Ming says, and that's what its customers seem to be.

Stuffing for a Century

A good thing about running a knishery is that there aren't lots of other knisheries. A bad thing about running a knishery is that people aren't looking for knisheries. But when they are looking for a knishery, which they may be in New York City, they're bound to end up at Yonah Schimmel's, which is good for them and for the knishery.

Yonah Schimmel—whose main sign says "Shimmel" although the name is usually spelled "Schimmel"—is pretty much *the* knishery in a city known for its knishes. And it pretty much deserves to be, considering that it's been selling knishes from the same store in that city for over a hundred years.

Like many famous New York foods, the classic New York knish got its start from Jewish immigrants living on the Lower East Side. But the knish never quite caught on in the same way as, say, the bagel. A century ago there were lots of knish sellers. Now Yonah stands nearly alone.

When you walk in, you might fleetingly wonder how it stands at all. Few stores in New York have remained as resolutely unchanged. It has not only its original ceiling and walls but also its original (or close to it) tables. The counter's wood frame has so many coats of paint it looks like white frosting.

Within that frame you'll see the big trays of golden brown knishes, none of which, to some visitors' surprise, are square. The most familiar knish today may be the kind that's square and fried, but at Yonah's, the only authentic knish is the kind that's round and baked.

Traditionally, it has a filling of potatoes or kasha, but it's now also filled with things like broccoli, sweet potatoes, or mushrooms. Yonah's, not wholly intransigent, has added flavors like jalapeño-and-cheddar, and dessert flavors including apple cheese, cherry cheese, chocolate cheese, and apple strudel.

You get to eat your knish at one of the white-and-red tables, and if you're lucky, you get to see more knishes arrive in the white-and-red dumbwaiter. The dumbwaiter tells you that Yonah's knishes come from the basement. It doesn't tell you where the first knishes came from. Nobody knows.

The knish is a version of a snack that's familiar in many cultures. Other versions include the pierogi, the samosa, the pasty, and the empanada. They're all essentially dough wrapped around a filling. They are members of the dumpling family. Some are closely related.

Knishes in some form may go back centuries in Europe. Knishes in Yonah's form go back one century here. They were a favorite of the Jewish workers who were arriving from Eastern Europe. Like many dumpling-family members, knishes were tasty, filling, and cheap.

In 1916 the *New York Times* reported on a "knish war" on Rivington Street. The report called an Austrian named Max Green "the originator of the great knish." It told of how a competitor had brought in cabaret shows to sell knishes, and how Green had retaliated by hiring an oompah band.

Green, the story said, later gave out prize coupons with his knishes, leading to apparently unforeseen consequences: "It is said that one ambitious knish eater, who was trying to get enough coupons to trade for a pocket knife, ate twenty knishes at a sitting and was carried home."

Still, no one knows for sure whether Green sold the first New York knish, and as far as Yonah Schimmel's is concerned, the one who did that was Yonah Schimmel.

Yonah has been referred to as a Bulgarian and a Romanian, and also as a rabbi, a Torah scribe, and a Talmudic scholar. One thing's for sure, says the store's proprietor, Ellen Anistratov: "He wanted to teach people spirituality, but there was no money in it."

To keep body and soul together, Yonah's wife started baking knishes, and Yonah sold them from a pushcart on Coney Island, Ellen says. Soon he moved his cart to the Lower East Side. This all happened in the 1890s, long before the Knish War of 1916.

Yonah opened a store across the street, and he moved to the current location in 1910. Some accounts have it that he ran the store with his cousin Joseph Berger until Joseph and his wife, Rose (Yonah's daughter), took over.

In any case, the knishery—a word attributed to Yonah—eventually went to Yonah's granddaughter, Lillian Berger. Ellen credits Lillian and Lillian's nephew Shelly "Sonny" Berger with keeping the knishes coming for much of the twentieth century.

In the sixties Izzy Finkelstein, a longtime waiter, told the press that Eleanor Roosevelt once came in to get a bag of knishes for Franklin. He was also quoted as saying, "On Sundays, rich people, very rich people, used to come in their cars and they would wait in line for hours to get in."

In the eighties Lillian opened a Yonah's takeout on the Upper East Side, but she abandoned that to give her full attention to the main store. And she helped ensure the store's future in 1979 when she hired a Ukrainian immigrant named Alex Volfman.

Alex took over in the nineties and was joined by Ellen, his daughter, who says that she represents the sixth generation of Schimmels. She dreams of spreading Yonah's knishes all over the world. Meanwhile, she keeps coming up with new flavors of knishes to spread.

She has put blank books on every table to collect her visitors' comments. The comments validate the store's policy of restraint. One patron wrote: "We are still coming here after 55 years!!" Another: "Just like the knishes of my younger days. Some things are better left unchanged."

Along with the unchanged knishes and the unchanged store, Yonah's has unchanged spirituality. "The main idea about Yonah Schimmel was that his connection was to God," Ellen says. "People have a knish and say, 'That's heaven!' So there is a connection there."

Appendix A:

FEATURED PLACES BY CATEGORY

Bakeries
De Robertis Pasticceria & Caffè, 41
The Donut Pub, 45
Glaser's Bake Shop, 73
Hungarian Pastry Shop, 89
Poseidon Greek Bakery, 153
Yonah Schimmel Knish Bakery, 197

Bars
Arthur's Tavern, 9
The Four Seasons, 61
Gallagher's Steak House, 65
Heidelberg Restaurant, 81
Keens Steakhouse, 105
McSorley's Old Ale House, 124
Old Town Bar, 141
P.J. Clarke's, 144
Rolf's German Restaurant, 157
Sardi's, 165
'21' Club, 185

Books
Argosy Book Store, 1
Strand Book Store, 176

Brassieres/Lingerie
Town Shop, 181

Burgers
Big Nick's Burger Joint & Pizza
   Joint, 21
Eisenberg's Sandwich Shop, 57
La Bonbonniere, 109
Lexington Candy Shop, 113
McSorley's Old Ale House, 124
Old Town Bar, 141
P.J. Clarke's, 144
Serendipity 3, 168

Cafes
Caffè Reggio, 28
De Robertis Pasticceria & Caffè, 41
Hungarian Pastry Shop, 89

Candy
Economy Candy, 53

Chinese Restaurants
Nom Wah Tea Parlor, 137
Wo Hop Restaurant, 193

Appendix B:

FEATURED PLACES BY NEIGHBORHOOD

Chelsea
The Donut Pub, 45

Chinatown
Nom Wah Tea Parlor, 137
Wo Hop Restaurant, 193

East Village
De Robertis Pasticceria & Caffè, 41
Gem Spa, 69
John's of 12th Street, 97
McSorley's Old Ale House, 124
Strand Book Store, 176

Flatiron
Eisenberg's Sandwich Shop, 57

Gramercy
Rolf's German Restaurant, 157

Greenwich Village
Café Reggio, 28
Native Leather, 133

Hell's Kitchen
Barbetta, 13
Chez Napoléon, 37
Poseidon Greek Bakery, 153

Lower East Side
Aron Streit, Inc., 5
Economy Candy, 53
Katz's Delicatessen, 100
Sammy's Roumanian Steak
 House, 161
Yonah Schimmel Knish Bakery, 197

Midtown East
Argosy Book Store, 1
The Four Seasons, 61
Grand Central Oyster Bar &
 Restaurant, 76
Marchi's Restaurant, 117
P.J. Clarke's, 144

Midtown West
Carnegie Delicatessen, 32
Gallagher's Steak House, 65
JJ Hat Center, 93

Appendix C:

FEATURED PLACES BY YEAR OF ORIGIN*

1854: McSorley's Old Ale House, 124

1884: P.J. Clarke's, 144

1885: Keens Steakhouse, 105

1888: Katz's Delicatessen, 100

1888: Town Shop, 181

1892: Old Town Bar, 141

1902: Glaser's Bake Shop, 73

1902: Heidelberg Restaurant, 81

1904: De Robertis Pasticceria & Caffè, 41

1906: Barbetta, 13

1908: Barney Greengrass, 17

1908: John's of 12th Street, 97

1910: Yonah Schimmel Knish Bakery, 197

1911: JJ Hat Center, 93

1913: Grand Central Oyster Bar & Restaurant, 76

1916: Aron Streit Inc., 5

1920: Nom Wah Tea Parlor, 137

1921: Sardi's, 165

1923: Poseidon Greek Bakery, 153

1925: Argosy Book Store, 1

1925: Lexington Candy Shop, 113

1925: Marie's Crisis Café, 121

1927: Caffè Reggio, 28

1927: Gallagher's Steak House, 65

1927: Gem Spa, 69

1927: Sammy's Roumanian Steak House, 161

1927: Strand Book Store, 176

1929: Eisenberg's Sandwich Shop, 57

1929: Marchi's Restaurant, 117

1929: '21' Club, 185

1932: La Bonbonniere, 109

1932: Papaya King, 149

1935: Village Vanguard, 189

1937: Arthur's Tavern, 9

1937: Carnegie Delicatessen, 32

1937: Economy Candy, 53

1938: Wo Hop Restaurant, 193

1951: Duplex, 49

1954: Serendipity 3, 168

1955: Café Carlyle, 25

1958: Music Inn World Instruments, 129

1958: The Silversmith, 173

1959: Native Leather, 133

1959: The Four Seasons, 61

1960: Chez Napoléon, 37

1961: Hungarian Pastry Shop, 89

1962: Big Nick's Burger Joint & Pizza Joint, 21

1962: House of Oldies, 85

1964: The Donut Pub, 45

1968: Rolf's German Restaurant, 157

*Some years are approximate.

Photo Credits

All photos by Wellington Lee except the following:

Page viii: Licensed by Shutterstock.com
Page 24:   The Carlyle, A Rosewood Hotel
Page 60:   Courtesy of the Four Seasons Restaurant
Page 64:   Courtesy of Gallagher's Steak House, photography by
              Atsushi Tomioka
Page 104:   Courtesy of Keens Steakhouse
Page 164:   Sardi's Enterprises Ltd.
Page 184:   '21' Club

Index